AGGIE SPIRIT 101

Howdy!
May God bless you always
with Greater Love!
and Dig 'Em!
Brother Barry

AGGIE SPIRIT 101

GREATER LOVE

BARRY BAUERSCHLAG

To order additional copies of this book, contact:
Xlibris
1-888-795-4274
www.Xlibris.com
Orders@Xlibris.com
548153

CONTENTS

Introduction ix

Chapter 1   Greater Love & the Spirit of Aggieland 1
Chapter 2   Christian Honor & the Aggie Ethic 16
Chapter 3   Christian Hospitality & "Howdy!" 35
Chapter 4   Christian Friendship & the Twelfth Man 50
Chapter 5   Ruth, Reveille, & Biblical, Zoological Psychology 69
Chapter 6   Honor Your Father and Mother &
            Appreciate Your Aggie Heritage 85
Chapter 7   Laborers for the Harvest & the Aggie Work Ethic 103
Chapter 8   The Role of Rituals & Importance of
            Aggie Traditions 118

Afterword 139

Champion Children Of God Song Book 144
Champion Children Of God 144
Greater Love 146
As Dawns The Day 148
Hear My Prayer, Lord 150
God, Our Father 151
TLC Prayer Song 152
A Family Prayer 153
Butterflies 153
Jesus Christ 154
Everything Grows With Love 154
Wash Me 155

Deep And Wide 155

Taste The Reign 156

All Day Song 157

Rejoice In The Lord Always 158

The Twenty-Third Psalm Song (Always) 159

God's Own Son 161

Sleep, Rest 162

Day Is Done 163

Christmas Story 164

O For A Heart To Praise My God 166

Mount Wesley 167

Reach One More 168

Seasons Of The Salvation Story 169

Seed Faith Song 170

A Christian Family 171

Rock-a My Soul 172

The Jesus Journey 173

Families For Shalom 174

Chosen By God 175

Appendices

FAITH 176

A Prayer of Encouragement 178

Practicing Powerful Prayer 180

Yell Practice Tips for the Twelfth Man 182

Aggie Spirit 101: Greater Love
    A Suggested Meeting Format Outline 184

My Prayer Journal 186

My Prayer Journal (continued) 187

Home Harvest Ministries of Aggieland 188

Fortieth A&M Reunion Prayer 189

Biblical Bipartisanship 190

Top Ten Reasons for the Big Event 192

Conflict Resolution..193
Christian Parenting 194
Honor–Shame Intensity Graph...197
The Story of Wesley Bauerschlag...199
Some Favorite Aggie Recipes... 202
An Introduction To The Last Corps Trip 203

ILLUSTRATIONS

SSgt Barry Sadler-Green Beret xi
Greater Love Heart Logo..........xv, 2, 8, 27, 28, 42, 62, 74, 94, 108, 134, 166,
181, 183, 188, 191
Bible...4
Football... 6, 7
Lawrence "Sul" Ross 16
Major General James Earl Rudder 17
Baseball..19
Ring Crest '70 .... 20, 59, 127
Ten Commandments Tablets......................23, 26, 86, 107
Lyre...24
Handshake 28, 37
E King Gill..50
Watering Can... 55, 105, 122, 170
Reveille...71
Cardinal..73
AMC Patch (Shield) 88
Original "Old Glory" 92
Corps Brass 130

Letters to Seth and Olivia, Deacon and Knox
on
The Christian Faith & The Traditions of Texas A&M

INTRODUCTION

I was probably preverbally "marooned"! And to help you better understand and trust what I will say to you in this book, I would like to share with you a little about from whence I come.

My dad, Walter Bauerschlag '50, played football for Texas A & M and head coach Homer Norton. Coach Norton's Aggies had won the national championship in 1939, and three Southwest Conference championships. While Dad was an All-District football hero at San Marcos High School, my mother was a/his cheerleader and Football Sweetheart. When Mom became pregnant with me right before his sophomore year, Dad decided to shift his focus to becoming a great husband/father and an exemplary civil engineering student. But Dad also was an outstanding Twelfth Man who tutored such football standouts as Bob Smith (who still holds the single game rushing record) and Glen Lippman (another Aggie running back in the Aggie Hall of Fame). These former teammates must have been grateful, and, along with other football players and Aggie friends, great Twelfth Men for me and my family as well, for they made a strong positive impression. A favorite keepsake which reminds me of their friendship is a silver baby spoon with my initials "BWB" given to me by the Aggie Football Team. Being "born with a silver spoon in one's mouth" is an expression of growing up in a life of privilege, meaning well moneyed, which I was not. But I was blessed to have grown up in an Aggie family, and that itself was a special privilege. And I know how deeply I have loved Texas A&M all of my life.

My mother's brother, Jim Barry '52, who had been a guitarist in the Aggie swing band and later served two tours as a US Army Officer advisor with Ranger status in Vietnam, was another early Aggie inspiration, mentor and role model. Like many other young people who sense something true and lasting in the ideals both spoken of in Aggie songs and many other traditions, and embodied in the brave and friendly, assertive and non-anxious leadership/friendship given by so many Aggie graduates, I felt a tremendous admiration and attraction to be a part of their great heritage, community, and place in history. I wanted to be an Aggie and Twelfth Man too!

So one of the happiest days of my life was in the spring of 1966 when I was accepted into Texas A & M University. I was a senior at Alamo Heights High School in San Antonio where I served on the Student Council, was President of the Slide Rule Club, and also had played football. My church youth group at St. Andrews Methodist Church elected me President of the Senior High MYF (Methodist Youth Fellowship). On graduation night I was gratefully surprised with one of three scholarships ($600 – a lot back then!) offered by the PTO.

I also was blessed to be one of the top math and science students in San Antonio (fish (then Phil) Frye of my outfit, F-1, another), and had prepared myself to be able to pursue engineering as my dad had. But I loved the Lord as well, having dedicated my life to be his disciple when I was confirmed as a sixth grader at the Methodist Church in New Braunfels, Texas by Reverend Ross Welch. And I was concerned about all the troubles and needs in the world around me: from the threat of global nuclear war and a raging conflict in Viet Nam, to a huge struggle by ethnic minorities for civil rights and equal opportunity, and the growing awareness that our ecological environment was being poisoned and polluted. The solutions seemed more spiritual than simply scientific; more ethical and political than just technological.

I felt tremendous appreciation for the love and guidance God had given me through my/His church with tremendous mentoring from people like my pastor, the Reverend Darrel Gray, St. Andrew Methodist Church, San Antonio. Our house was next door to the parsonage, and I admired these spiritual leaders and their families. I also loved the arts and social sciences as well, having sung in the church choir and taught myself (with the help of my brother Bobby) to play the guitar. When I was in junior high I had been given an art scholarship at La Villita near old downtown San Antonio where I studied painting. So when at seventeen my beloved associate pastor Ted Spellman talked with me about going into ministry I felt both affirmed and befuddled, tempted and torn. I sensed a lack of immediate support from my family for a career in ministry, especially from my dad. They were less naive about the cross I would have to bear. My mother eventually came to connect my decision for ministry with the traditional vocations of education/coaching/school administration and medical physicians of her father, grandfather, and great grandfathers. Dad suggested that if I wasn't sure, it would be prudent to have secured hours of coursework in engineering which could transfer to another major. To transfer non-engineering courses back to engineering would not be as possible. To further complicate things, the Vietnam War was cranking up, and with a low draft number I much preferred to be a commissioned officer from A & M than a private. But I guess mainly I was just happy to be becoming an Aggie, and trusted God to help me figure things out as time went on. So in the fall of 1966 I was excited, overjoyed, and a little anxious as I reported as an engineering freshman student/cadet at Texas A & M, and a fish in Company F-1, "Finest First"!

Life in the Corps of Cadets at Texas A & M in the late 1960's was extremely challenging, but ultimately very rewarding. Even with my background relationship to Aggieland I had no real idea what I had gotten myself into! As a young Christian and leader of my church youth group I had made promises and commitments that seemed in danger of becoming lost in the rigorous, stressful world into which I had stepped! I lost ten pounds which I really didn't have to lose those first few weeks, from 155 to 145. I was forced to listen to and use language to which I was not accustomed, and to perform acts which before I would have been too embarrassed, anxious and self-conscious to perform. To say I was stretched beyond my imagination just to survive, much less thrive would have been an understatement! My thoughts about leaving or quitting were not just because it was so hard, but because much of these new demands seemed to go against my beliefs and commitments as a Christian! But I "kept on keeping on", "one day at a time", and needless now to say I did survive. And as time went by, I could begin counting the blessings that came with "enduring and long-suffering"! I grew stronger and more independent, and more interdependent. And I am now as an adult very thankful for the encouragement that Dad gave me when he explained that throughout my life I would find myself in the position of being a freshman. He said that if I would just "tough it out" through my fish year at A & M, I would be confidently able to meet all future rookie challenges. And guess what! I came to learn he was right! As Mark Twain wisely and humorously noted, it is amazing how much more I realized my father knew as I have gotten older, more mature, and wiser myself!

When I finally came to the end of my freshman year, to my surprise I was named the Outstanding Freshman (Best Drilled) of my outfit, and selected to be an assistant squad leader (Cadet Corporal) for my sophomore year. My perseverance was paying off with new honors, responsibilities, friendships, experiences and privileges in the meritocracy of Texas A&M! Historically, "Pinkie" Wilson, who wrote the Aggie War Hymn and inspired me and generations of Aggies with his enthusiasm for God and Aggieland, passed on in the spring of that freshman year. His memorial service as was Earl Rudders three years later was held from A&M Methodist Church. Maturation is a process of choosing beliefs and molding character through prayer with many varied experiences of desperation, inspiration, and perspiration.

I continued to learn a lot my sophomore year as an Assistant Squad Leader with new challenges and responsibilities, which helped me grow in my confidence and courage. One thing I learned was that my "gung ho" idealism may have been too demanding on the handful of fish given to me for training, and I regretted their departure after that year.

My junior year I was asked to serve as the Scholastic Sergeant on First Brigade Staff, and also was selected to be in the Ross Volunteers. Though on staff, I continued to connect to my outfit, and support my buddies and other members. My leadership was also challenged, demonstrated, and recognized at Army summer camp that next summer at Fort Sill, Oklahoma.

My senior year I was privileged to be asked to serve as the first Commanding Officer of Company L-1, Lone Star Company (the better half of Company F-1;-)! I also was elected by my RV peers to be on the Firing Squad for my senior year. As a Ross Volunteer I was honored to serve Texas Governor Preston Smith at his inauguration, and also to honor President

Earl Rudder with a twenty-one gun salute at his funeral the spring of my senior year.

As I have gone through my adult life as a pastor and minister of the Gospel of Jesus Christ and the United Methodist Church, and as the father of two fine Aggie sons, and as family to quite numerous Aggie brothers and sisters, nieces, nephews, cousins, and church members, I have come to see even more that the benefits and blessings of Texas A&M and becoming an Aggie are much more than just academic and practical. They are indeed spiritual, moral and theological as well! It is an education that includes building character along with competency. It is growing in truth and love with training and leadership. It is education as it should be done, but often, especially nowadays, gets neglected.

After marrying a sweet, local Sicilian/Italian-American Bryan girl, Donna Kaye Santana, graduating as a distinguished student in Mechanical Engineering, and being commissioned as an Army officer, I served both as an engineer with Brown and Root, Inc. and as an Army Ordinance officer in Maryland and Virginia during the Vietnam War. I was honorably discharged a few months early in order that I start seminary. With the help of the GI Bill I went to Perkins School of Theology at SMU (Southern Methodist University). As a first year student/seminarian (freshman again!☺) I was challenged by my Phenomenology of Religion professor, Dr. Fred Streng to do a term paper/project on the "religion of Texas A & M". In other words he wanted me to describe the ultimate concerns and claims embraced by the traditions of A & M. That is, he wanted me to try and show what the underlying nature and purpose of the rules, rituals, and reasons of the Aggie culture were about. I was at that time however quite interested in the "self actualization/personal growth", and "small group movements". And because I also sensed much less than respect, even disdain for A & M and its "cultic customs" from this professor (and many other "non-Aggies"), I chose the latter topics for my term report. But his challenge to interpret and define the religion of Texas A&M always haunted me.

During many years of pastoral ministry, including a couple of years doing Doctor of Ministry coursework (again at Perkins, SMU), I continued to study what it is about God's Spirit in a faith community which is creative, redemptive, and sustaining. Especially helpful were the study/experiences in family enrichment (parenting, marriage enrichment, couples communication theory, family systems theory, human sexuality, life stages, etc.), youth ministries, counselling and addiction recovery ministries.

I also went through concurrently many years of supporting the Aggie community. I offered Class Reunion invocations, and Aggie Muster speeches and prayers. I attended football and other sports events. Four of my younger siblings went through A&M, while my oldest sister married one of my classmates and outfit buddies, Max Melcher. But especially as I supported our oldest son Jason, (who was the Fund Raising Chairperson for the Class of '94, and graduated President of the student body from A & M's Medical School), then literally followed our son Matt '99 and the Aggie Band through his four years there (where he played trombone and gave leadership as a member of the Bugle Rank and Commander of A Battery and was finally named the outstanding Aggie Band senior for the Class of '99), I came to feel the need, yes, even the call to write down my thoughts: about the shared values of the Christian faith (and indeed other quality theologies) and the traditional, spiritual heritage of Texas A & M University.

Many Aggies, both old Ag buddies and young Ag students have told me that they would love to read and recommend such a book. I am most grateful for their encouragement to get it written. I believe that though there are so many spiritually dedicated Aggies of leadership (such as Frank *"I Bleed Maroon"* Cox with whom I have shared Aggie friendship and Muster leadership) that God has uniquely equipped me to offer this book for insight and inspiration. And though the Aggie Spirit is "a Spirit can ne'er be told", I know there is a desire from many to better understand this Spirit. Certainly there is experience and education that equips some of us to more fully share the nature of this Spirit. Indeed, God's truth and grace is admittedly amazing and mysterious, profound and mystical! And so it is with humility and honor, reverence and experience that I approach this project. I want these words to invoke reflection and discussion. For I hope this book will better equip you and your Aggie friends/family with Christian passion and purpose, with Aggie fire and fight!

And last but not least is my motivation of greater love and higher hope that I have for my grandchildren. Seth and Olivia are by my oldest son Jason and daughter-in-law Janua '95, and Deacon and Knox by my younger son Matt and daughter-in-law Heather. They have made me very thankful and extremely proud! I include as well my nieces, nephews, cousins, and all future generations of Aggies! My prayers and blessings are deeply for those in the Corps of Cadets and the Fightin' Texas Aggie Band. Especially do I love and admire all the Aggie athletes and student Twelfth Men who loyally support them. Last, but not least do I treasure the sincere love in wise guidance of my Aggie Mom and Dad, in the blessings from beloved grandparents and great (times ___) grandparents. To these and all Aggies who want to be greater Christians AND greater Aggies I dedicate this book.

I am truly humbled as I undertake this endeavor. And my prayer as I set out to write this is that it will continue to help encourage and educate the Aggie family about our shared ideals for excellence, integrity, honor, hospitality, service, loyalty, and leadership for Texas A&M, *"Building Champions"* who are "more than conquerors" for our churches, and our great state, nation, and world.

God bless you with greater love, and gig 'em,

Barry W. Bauerschlag '70

Notes

My senior Aggieland photo.

As a young lieutenant in my dress blues with Donna at officer's social at Ft. Lee, Virginia.

Welcoming Governor Preston Smith (with President Earl Rudder to his right) with a Ross Volunteer saber arch. Son, Matt '99, provided the same to the newly elected Gov. George W. Bush.

Leading Company L-1 on our Corps Trip to Houston to play Rice.

My Student Days
I was humbled and honored to be
asked to lead the new outfit Company
L-1, Lonestar Company as a senior,
and to have our photo introduce the
Aggieland's Corps of Cadets section.

Cadet Major Barry Bauerschlag
Commanding Officer of L-1. The
senior boots had belonged to Jim
Cartwright of Second Brigade
Staff who was later killed in
Vietnam.

1966-67 fish Bauerschlag of Company F-1, Finest First

This "Heritage Corner" of our living room recalls the past with honor and the future with hope. I inherited my grandfather's roll-top desk after my dad passed on in 1985. Their management/leadership skills and discipline are a continuing inspiration. Framed poster "101 Ways to Praise a Child" point to parenting leadership responsibilities. That "Everything Grows with Love" is evidenced by Matt's RV Firing Squad and Band Bugle Rank photo. Our "Ring Dance" photo and L-1 Commanding Officer saber rest on the desk. A maroon candle helps symbolize the warmth and wisdom, light and love of the Spirit!

A handmade gift from one of the new couples, Debbie and Carl Johnson in the New Covenant Sunday School Class Donna and I started in Harlingen First United Methodist Church in 1976, Debbie's handmade gift became a theme of my ministry. My sons, Jason and Matt helped write a song by that title (See Champion Children of God Songbook in the Appendices). (The water can is an agricultural symbol of the Twelfth Man ministry of nurture: honor, support and encouragement.)

As the SWT Conference Youth Retreat Director at Mt Wesley in Kerrville, I first designed this heart/fish/cross logo for the theme, "The Power of Love". The towels, later autographed by each small group (CFU-Camp Family Unit) were a symbol of discipleship servanthood, and used the last morning as we shared communion and washed each other's feet. This was sort of an early version of the 12th Man Towel; a precursor symbol of unselfish service. (Note; Ja SON autograph).

Summer work as a deckhand in Alaska off Anchorage in Cook Inlet (wearing my "F-1 Finest First" sweatshirt) after my fish year.

And in the Gulf of Mexico on a pipe-laying barge as a welder helper. Helping pay our way through college is an important tradition.

Receiving "Best Drilled" Medal/ Ribbon as a Freshman in 1967 from my C. O. Dwight Recht of Company F-1, "Finest First".

And with my Aggie Mom, Maybeth Barry Bauerschlag by our dorm, R. W. Briggs Hall. It was May 14, 1967, Mother's Day and my nineteenth birthday.

With my fish Ol' Lady, fish (Ross) Parish. Ross and 50% of our F-1 fish did not make it past their freshman year at A&M. Ross was a good 12th Man to me as fish Ol' Ladies should be. Thanks Ross!

As a junior (Scholastic Sergeant) on First Brigade staff with (l to r) Don Kidd, Bob Harding, and Tom Hoysa. I handpainted the sign during the summer (as I also designed and painted the L-1 Lonestar Company sign that next summer.

Consequences. With First Brigade C.O. Fred Blumberg and X.O. Greg Wren. I think I did more pushups as a junior RV with a wisecracking, jarhead frog Ol' Lady (Tom Hoysa)! (They saw a sign on my bulletin board "Down with Zippers", a nickname for seniors.)

*Final Review 1969
with First Brigade
Staff.*

*Ross Volunteer
Juniors of First
Brigade Staff:
Robert Harding,
myself (Barry
Bauerschlag), and
Tom Hoysa.*

*Aggies honoring
the past, yet
welcoming
progressive
change. This real
estate near the NE
corner of campus
after implosion of
this dated facility
is now filled
with excellent
student housing
and amenities!
Growing, building,
and leading for a
better tomorrow!*

CHAPTER 1

GREATER LOVE & THE
SPIRIT OF AGGIELAND

Howdy! Congratulations on choosing to read Aggie Spirit 101: Greater Love! Perhaps you are a youth who aspires to follow a family tradition, attends Texas A&M, and wants to discover even more of this community and its rich traditions. Or maybe you are a first-generation Aggie who is hungry to assimilate and nurture qualities you've admired in other Aggies. It could be you've already graduated from A&M and would like to refresh and better understand the values you've learned there, as well as learn how to translate them more effectively into your present life challenges. As you mature in your life as an Aggie, you probably seek a more holistic and integrated spirituality. Chances are you would like to better understand the scriptural foundations for your faith. You may desire to perceive a healthy partnership or synergy between the Holy Spirit and the Aggie Spirit. Maybe even discover how God's Spirit is the true Aggie Spirit!

As a serious and sincere Christian since my youth, these are concerns that have propelled me to explore how to become a better Christian and a good Aggie at the same time. It has been my privilege to have lived my life close to the traditions of both the church and Texas A&M and to be called upon for leadership in both communities. So after over forty years in the ordained ministry and a lifetime of being an Aggie, and though "there's a Spirit can ne'er told," I believe that I may be as qualified to try as anybody is. Wherever you are in your life's journey, my hope and prayer is that this book/course will offer you insight and inspiration, as well as give you invitation to closer friendships with those who follow Christ and who also

1

claim the name "Aggie." The effectiveness of this book will increase as you seek to discuss and apply it with a study group that meets over a period of several weeks. Aggie Spirit 101: Greater Love is ultimately a faith statement offered to encourage you, the reader, toward a greater life.

The foundation of the Christian faith is the witness of the God of Jesus Christ by his word and actions. At the heart of his gospel is his example of a life of loyal love and personal faith in God that offers peace, hope, and joy and brings transformation to those who trust him. The love all faithful followers are invited to embrace is a true love that is unconditional, bringing blessings to those who believe and act upon his word. It is also an unselfish love willing to sacrifice and has shown itself most purely on the cross of Calvary.

Love and our invitation to faith, to trust and follow, is Jesus's priority. When asked which was the greatest commandment, He answered, "Love the Lord your God with all your heart, and with all your soul, and with all your mind. This is the greatest and first commandment, And a second is like it: 'You shall love your neighbor as yourself.' On these two commandments hang all the Law and the Prophets" (Matthew 22:37–40).

In the Epistles of John, we are also reminded of the crucial character of love: "We should love one another. We must not be like Cain who was from the evil one and murdered his brother" (1 John 3:11b–12a). "Little children, let us love, not in word or speech, but in truth and action" (1 John 3:18). "Beloved, let us love one another, because love is from God; everyone who loves is born of God and knows God. Whoever does not love does not know God, for God is love. God's love was revealed among us in this way: God sent his only Son into the world so that we might live through him. In this is love, not that we loved God, but that he loved us and sent his Son to be the atoning sacrifice for our sins. Beloved, since God loved us so much, we also ought to love one another. No one has ever seen God; if we love one another, God lives in us, and his love is perfected in us" (1 John 4:7–12). "God is love, and those who abide in love abide in God, and God abides in them. Love has been perfected among us in this: that we may have boldness on the day of judgment, because as he is, so are we in this world" (John 4:16b–17). "We love because he first loved us. Those who say, 'I love God,' and hate their brothers and sisters, are liars; for those who do not love a brother or sister whom they have seen, cannot love God whom they have not seen. The commandment we have from him is this: those who love God must love their brothers and sisters also" (1 John 4:19–21).

In the famous Thirteenth Chapter of Saint Paul's first letter to the church in Corinth (often called "The Love Chapter"), Paul begins by boldly declaring that love is essential: "If I speak in the tongues of mortals and of angels, but do not have love, I am a noisy gong or a clanging cymbal. And if I have prophet powers, and understand all mysteries and all knowledge, and if I have all faith so as to remove mountains, but do not have love, I am nothing. If I give away all my possessions, and if I hand over my body so that I may boast, but do not have love, I gain nothing." No matter what else we have or do, if we do not have love, we are simply ineffective or insignificant. Love is what makes life work! Love is what makes life matter! Without love, everything is for naught! Love is essential.

Paul goes on to explain the nature of love: "Love is patient; love is kind; love is not envious or boastful or arrogant or rude. It does not insist on its own way; it is not irritable or resentful; it does not rejoice in wrongdoing, but in the truth. It bears all things, believes all things, hopes all things, endures all things. Love never ends" (1 Corinthians 13:4–8a). Paul then contrasts that picture with the image of childishness and immaturity. He explains that we must learn the art of loving and that maturity takes time, study, practice, and discipline. And it helps to have the encouragement of other pilgrims on this spiritual journey.

Paul concludes this beautiful "Love Chapter" with another strong affirmation of faith, "And now faith, hope and love abide, these three; and the greatest of these is love" (1 Corinthians 13:13). Can there be any doubt for Christians about what is most important? Is it any wonder that so many couples choose these verses for their weddings, as foundational statements for their new families, as my wife Donna and I did? And, of course, this scripture talks about not only the romantic love between a husband and wife but also the true love that binds and blesses all our relationships. This godly love that endures for better or worse, for richer or poorer, in sickness and in health is the true love that welcomes an abundant home harvest! (Thus the name of my ministry.)

In John's gospel, we hear, "No one has greater love than this, to lay down one's life for one's friends" (John 15:13). Love has many languages or ways of expressing itself: service, physical affection, words/signs of affirmation/appreciation, active listening, gift giving, sharing quality time, etc. But the greatest expression of love was and is shown in its sacrificial acts for those we love.

With the acceptance through faith of this powerful love of God (the church has called it "grace" or "agape" love) comes redemption, salvation, and the gift of new, joyful, abundant, free, and eternal life. This is true not just for individuals, but also and especially for groups such as families, teams, military outfits, and schools. These all become part of the larger community of believers the Christian community calls the church, biblically the *"eklesia"*. Some prioritize other principles and values such as trusting money, power or control, pleasure and thrills, and popularity and fame. But God's true love brings true life only to those with the faith to follow, to put faith and love first. Jesus said, "What will it profit them to gain the whole world and forfeit their life?" (Mark 8:36). Indeed, Jesus speaks of a different profit/prophet motive! He is speaking of the paradoxical nature of steadfast love when it demonstrates itself in sacrificial acts. "For those who want to save their life will lose it, and those who lose their life for my sake, and for the sake of the Gospel will save it" (Mark 8:35). God's grace results in victorious living for those who believe and embrace Him through faith in His Son and His unselfish service to others. Trusting the truth and grace of Christ brings healing and help to the wounded of this world: the blind gain their sight, the deaf can hear, the lame can walk, the shamed are made clean, the dead are raised, and the poor given hope (see Matthew 11:5).

In other words, this love of God in Christ is meant for ministry, making a difference, not just in the life of the one who receives it, but also through that person to others. It can be likened to the life-giving waters of the Jordan River near Jesus's earthly home of Galilee. This life-giving river flows into and out of Lake Gennesaret (means harp or the same shape; also known as the Sea of Galilee), which abounds with life. The lake provides abundant food (mainly fish) to many around it. But this same water, which a little farther south flows only into but not out of the Dead Sea, becomes too salty to support any life. Like the fresh water of the Jordan River, the overflowing gift of God's grace is meant to be passed on through us to those around us, bringing and sustaining life. True love, God's greater love, is shared love.

At the climax and conclusion of his ministry, Jesus simplifies spirituality and religious ethics when he gives his disciples his new commandment, "Love one another!" He then qualifies what he means by that commandment when he adds, "As I have loved you, so you should love one another" (John 13:34).

Throughout the New Testament, the love command is further explained with other "one anothers," such as "encourage one another, honor one another, be kind to one another, forgive one another, bear one another's burdens, pray for one another, build one another up, etc." By living this way, we enjoy the righteousness or right relationship that God desires and requires. This is the priority that we are challenged to pursue as Jesus taught in the Sermon on the Mount, "Strive first for the Kingdom of God and his righteousness and all these things will be given to you as well" (Matthew 6:33). This is my witness as a confirmed Christian since I was twelve and an ordained minister since 1973.

It is also my witness as an old Ag that this greater love is the essence of what it means to be an Aggie. It is my proclamation to all you young Ags (and not-so-young Ags) that this is the ideal that is embraced in all of Texas A&M's finest traditions. The truths of these traditions are about treasured values that bring honor to God, oneself, the Aggie family or nation, and those they serve. These are the precious merits that the A&M community has prized and that opens the door and welcomes the blessings of joy, hope, and prosperity (heavenly riches and "mammon = worldly pleasures/wealth," if it is not served [a false god or idol if so], but used to serve God and others).

5

I love to witness to this power of God's steadfast love, which does "endure forever." One of my favorite stories is about the football season of 1967. It was my sophomore year, and (without being sophomoric) the Aggies were expected to have a great year after ten years of getting outscored a lot. One popular joke was that it had gotten so bad that the tradition was adjusted, so as to kiss your date on first downs instead of touchdowns! It had been ten years since we had beaten t.u. or competed seriously for a championship. That was a decade since Coach Bear Bryant and his "Junction Boys" contended and conquered so well in Aggieland. And now, Gene Stallings, one of the Junction Boys, was in his third year as our head coach. A popular bumper sticker read, "The Aggies Are Back!" But after the first four games, our record was 0–4, and some folks were inserting the word "way" on that bumper sticker, as in "The Aggies Are Way Back." (There have always been "two-percenters" who don't believe.) But our great student leadership under the direction of our yell leaders held an impromptu yell practice in the rain (wonderful metaphor for the Aggies situation)! It was at the football players' dorm the night before they left for Lubbock and their away game with Texas Tech. We let the team (of which we were a part as Twelfth Men) know that we knew that they weren't giving up and that we weren't giving up on them! We stood in the rain for about an hour and showed them our support with steadfast love, honor, and encouragement. We were "down; the going was rough and tough," but "we just grinned and yelled, 'We've got the stuff to fight together'"! It was a great yell practice!

After driving all the way to Lubbock to see the game and a girlfriend (in that order), I remember standing at the game in the cold of the High Plains, amid a sea of unwelcoming Red Raiders as the Aggie football team fought a hard battle in a close game. As the clock ran down, the Aggies found themselves behind by a few points, but with the ball and driving toward the end zone. Our quarterback, Edd Hargett, was a great passer and leader of our team, but the abuse from getting hit in the pocket left him with a brace on each knee and diminished mobility. At the Tech twenty-five-yard line, Edd dropped back for one last chance, only to find all of his receivers covered. He then tucked the ball and began to run for it. Talk about needing a miracle! It was indeed prayer time! Then Larry Stegent, our halfback, made an amazing block of two Red Raider defenders that took them out and cleared the way. And after the clock had run out, Edd Hargett crossed the goal line at the right corner of the end zone for the winning touchdown! What a display of the Spirit's "awesome magic" and testimony to "greater love"! But the story was not over. The Aggies continued to trust, grow in faith, and fight throughout the season. They continued to make prayer-blessed, unlikely third- and fourth-down plays: long passes from Hargett to Tommy Maxwell and Bob Long; determined runs by Wendell Housely and Larry Stegent. There were crucial blocks from Jack Kovar, Tom Buckman, Mike Caswell, Rolf Kreuger, Walter Mohn, and Billy Kubecka. Booming kicks from Steve O'Neal. And how about the key defensive stops from Billy Hobbs, Harvey Aschenbeck, Curley Hallman, and Grady Allen. The whole team fought valiantly: too many to name here. And the victories followed, until they beat t.u. on Thanksgiving Day and were headed to the Cotton Bowl as Southwest Conference Champions! There they even defeated the Bear Bryant–coached Crimson Tide of Alabama!

In the Gospel of John, Jesus declares, "I am the (true) vine, you are the branches. Those who abide in me and I in them bear much fruit, because apart from me you can do nothing" (John 15:5). There indeed is a rich harvest for those who abide in this true love, whether as traditional Christians or as true Aggies faithful to each other and to A&M's traditions and higher values. God is a loving father whose joy is to bless His children with many good gifts. Just as a human father delights in bringing blessings to his children and watching them do well, even more does our heavenly Father rejoice in our righteousness and in giving us through faith an abundant, prosperous, and victorious life. In Luke's Gospel, we hear Jesus promise that our reward will be great when we embrace and enact God's mercy and grace (see Luke 6:35–36). And, "The good person out of the good treasures of the heart produces good" (Luke 6:45a). Then also we read, "Forgive, and you will be forgiven; give, and it will be given to you. A good measure, pressed down, shaken together, running over, will be put into your lap; for the measure you give will be the measure you get back" (Luke 6:37b–38). This home harvest describes the heart of the gospel or good news of Jesus Christ and the happiness of living out the life of greater love.

Notes

Chapter 1

Suggested Questions for Reflection, Discussion, and Sharing

1. If home is where we feel loved, how does Aggieland feel like the "home of the Twelfth Man" for you?

2. When did being an Aggie feel like being part of a family for you?

3. What are some of the experiences when traditions of Aggie friendliness made you feel at home?

4. Which scripture speaks best to you about love and its place in your life? In the Spirit of Aggieland?

5. What are some of the philosophies and their sayings that tempt you to trust something besides Greater Love, e.g., greed, control, lust, pleasure, thrills, escape or isolation, popularity, etc.?

6. How does sharing love not deplete the love you have received, but grow and strengthen it (like the Sea of Galilee)?

7. How is Jesus's commandment and explanation, "As I have loved you, so you should love one another" exciting for you? Scary?

8. What is the difference between serving mammon (worldly riches) and using mammon to serve God?

9. How does the 2012 football season remind you of 1967 and the story I shared? How is the faith journey a growing "Wow!"?

10. The Bible offers us the hope of an abundant harvest, an agricultural image/metaphor. What are some characteristics of this hope and dream for your life at this present point in your life?

Everything Grows with Greater Love.

The 2008 A&M Softball team's success was a team effort/ support by All-American's Jaimi Hinshaw (3B) and Jami Lobprise (OF) local standout Bailey Schroeder (OF), Holly Ridley (OF) wearing their Super Regional Champs T-shirts and young left-handed second baseman Natalie Villareal.

Holly Ridley

Natalie Villareal

Jami Lobpries

Jamie Hinson

Bailey Schroeder
(local A&M
Consolidated H.S.)

Three time All American Megan
Gibson, Aggie Softball Team,
pitcher/first base/legend after
winning the Super Regional in
College Station on the way to the
World Series (as #5 seed) and
National Championship games
in 2008. Named by Aggieland
Illustrated as Sportsperson of the
year (and just short of National
Player of the Year. She earned
Big 12 Pitcher and Player of
the Year - a first time combo) and
rewrote A&M and Big 12 record
books with homeruns and wins,
and with faith, determination, and
inspirational leadership led the
Aggies to greatness.

After the last volleyball game of 2013 our very successful team celebrated Senior Day with their outstanding and outgoing upperclassmen leaders.

Laurie and John Corbelli celebrate their season with one of their star volleyball students, Kelsey Black '12.

Honor is bestowed on the 2013 Aggie Volleyball team as Athletic Director Eric Hyman presents them in Reed Arena in recognition of their outstanding accomplishments. Encouraging excellence by appreciating accomplishment is one of A&M's finest traditions of honor.

Donna and I bought two of these Heisman collages wall hangings as Christmas gifts for both our sons, for office or home.

The "Power of 12" became also the "Power of 2"! Fear the Farmers! Fear the Thumb! Fear Johnny Football!

Here, the scoreboard and fireworks at Kyle Field celebrate the Aggie Football Team's 700th win.

This backyard bench from the limestone steps of the Richard Coke Building provides a steady anchor to the landscape, and the Governor's Opening Address words to our lives, "Let HONOR be your guiding star"!

2012, a special football season in Aggieland, was celebrated in a special way on 12/12/2012, as Johnny "Football" Manziel had just been voted the Heisman Award winner. It was an honor shared by the whole team, including the important "player", the 12th Man. Outside, and afterward inside the Memorial Student Center with the Trophy Aggies from all over shared in the glory and joy of this special season of victories.

Senior Spencer Neely and team mates standing near us gave "off the field" leadership and support as well to the festivities.

Johnny Manziel addressed the crowd on 12/12/12 after he received the Heisman.

CHAPTER 2

CHRISTIAN HONOR & THE AGGIE ETHIC

A well-known quotation at Texas A&M is, "Let honor be your guiding star." First spoken by founding governor of Texas Richard Coke at A&M's opening on October 4, 1876, these words began, "Let your watchword be duty, and know no other talisman of success than labor. Let honor be your guiding star in your dealings with superiors, your fellows, with all. Be as true to a trust reposed as the needle to the pole; stand by the right even to the sacrifice of life itself, and learn that death is preferable to dishonor." Since the early 50s, these words are inscribed on the Coke Building just east of the Simpson Drill Field and between the field and the statue of Lawrence Sullivan Ross. These words were better exemplified for Aggies by Ross.

As a man of honor, Ross was known and is remembered as a "soldier, statesman, and knightly gentleman." Sul Ross (as he was called) was also a governor of Texas and president of the Agricultural and Mechanical College of Texas. Before that, he had served as a protector of pioneers from renegade Indians, a brigadier general during the Civil War, a farmer/rancher, sheriff of McLennan County (where his family had founded Waco), and a state senator. The courage, compassion, faith, and integrity that he exhibited in all his leadership inspired followers and support throughout his life. He was a hero and role model for many in the Lone Star State and beyond, then, and still today. His statue stands tall in front of the academic building and at the heart of the campus.

Each morning as I put on my Aggie ring, I look at its bold, lone large star, and renew my commitment to the honor of unchanging values in my life, which I call Jesus Christ, reaffirming the honor of knowing, following, and serving Him. It is a ritual of covenant renewal, a personal tradition of recommitment to righteousness. And as such, it brings the blessings of honor, common to both Christian discipleship and Texas A&M. For Jesus Christ is my primary hero and role model, my guiding star, and the source of all honor and glory. And this honor is also at the heart of what it means to be an Aggie.

The company of outstanding cadet upperclassmen, which serve as the honor guard of the governor of Texas, are named the Ross Volunteers (RVs), after Lawrence Sullivan Ross. They serve at state inaugurations to honor the newly elected heads of state. They also serve at Silver Taps and Aggie Muster to honor those Aggies who have recently passed on. That tradition started after President Ross died January 3, 1898, while in his eighth year as president of Texas AMC. A twenty-one gun RV salute honored him and his leadership contributions.

It was my sad honor and privilege at several of these bereavement ceremonies also to help fire the twenty-one gun salute. These included the car accident death of All-Conference Defensive MVP, defensive end Mike DeNiro and later another legendary, landmark president of Texas A&M, Major General James Earl Rudder. I am humbled and thankful to have been a part of that man and moment. But each person and Aggie is important and valued, with the human dignity of being made in God's likeness or image. Each Aggie who died that year was honored: those of campus at Silver Taps and Muster; those around the world at their local musters.

The Ross Volunteers or "RVs" as they are affectionately known (I also heard "yellow-throated quad trotters") are chosen from the larger cadet population under several criteria: leadership, integrity/character, and grades, but most certainly for embracing the Aggie Code of Honor. That is the noble tradition they are most expected to keep and exemplify.

The Aggie Code of Honor is brief, but big: "An Aggie does not lie, cheat, or steal, or tolerate those who do." Aggies understand that honorable character is inseparable from honorable behavior. To feel honorable and be a person of honor is to act with honor. In the movie "Forrest Gump," Forrest refutes being labeled "stupid" by quoting his mother as saying, "Stupid is as stupid does!" We might claim the corollary, "Honor is as honor does"! The Aggie Code of Honor calls all Aggies to an ideal of respect and responsibility toward others. It begins with honesty and a commitment to the truth. That means avoiding half-truths and distortions, as well as bold-faced lies. Character and credibility crumble when we fail to be truthful for truthful leads to trustful. An Aggie does not lie.

The second part of our code prohibits cheating, for cheating is a form of lying. Cheating is dishonesty, not with our words, but with our actions. My mother used to say, "A cheater never wins, and a winner never cheats!" and "Teasips might cheat, but Aggies were better than that." Changing their orange uniforms to the "burnt orange" color of the "pigskin" football seemed to me at the time to be an example of their deceit. Numerous bad calls by the refs that seemed too common were another example of cheating. Aggies play hard and are shrewd (with prowess bold!), but they aim to play fair!

A pastor was concerned that his church's softball team was struggling and losing most of their games. So he visited one of their practices and noticed that their equipment was worn, limited, and sadly lacking. He went back to the congregation and asked for donations. After collecting a hundred dollars, he presented it to the coach, telling him to spend it on whatever would help his team the most to win. Soon they started winning their games! And when the pastor saw the team again, he congratulated them. But he didn't see any new equipment! So he asked the coach how he had used the funds. The coach replied, "Well, you told me to spend it on whatever would help us to win, so I gave it to the umpire!"

Of course, any success built on anything less than honesty and integrity is hollow and fleeting. Cheaters don't really win. One of the areas in sports where cheating is a temptation and problem in recent times is in the use or abuse of dangerous steroids or growth hormones. The Aggies' and Christian ideal is to lean not on performance-enhancing drugs, but on performance-enhancing "hugs," the support of the Twelfth Man, and the grace/power of the Spirit! God promises and delivers! This support, which honors and energizes, is what has enabled countless Aggies to achieve extraordinary performances on the field and in so many different fields. These "playing fields and battle fields" have witnessed heroic service that has inspired and made a difference at many levels: personal, family, community, national, and world, in both civilian and military endeavors. Greater love leads to victorious living and the honor that goes with it!

The third prohibition in the Aggie code of honor is to not steal. That is to respect others' belongings and not take what does not belong to you. That includes inheritances, usury (unreasonably large interest on loans), or falsely destroying people's reputation, peace of mind, confidence, health, family, etc. That which is not yours: don't take it! Lives matter and property matters!

The Bible is a history of the honor/glory of God's greater truth and love. Throughout time, God has been active in creation and re-creation, in redeeming the lives of His creatures and children, pointing the way toward abundant and eternal life, and sustaining us along the journey. Out of the great faithfulness of His amazing grace, God has been about the work of deliverance from many dangers, toils, and snares. His loyal love has resulted in the transformation of so many lives with real healing and hope! Story after story in the Bible tells us of this awesome power of the Almighty to save.

Let us begin at the beginning. In the first book of the Bible, Genesis, it says that with truth and grace, God breathed His *ruah* over the face of the chaos and darkness and spoke his word, "Let there be light!" *Ruah* is the Hebrew word that translates as "wind or breath or spirit." In this case, all three apply and indicate an intimate experience of God's loving favor. Combined with the powerful word of God, giving meaning and purpose to the experience of God's love, the transformation we call creation began. It is this same combination of grace and truth, love and law, affection and definition, warmth and wisdom that is operative throughout the Bible and the history of our lives.

In the New Testament, thousands of years later, Jesus would most clearly reveal this process in the New Creation called redemption. He would embody and show the steadfast love of the Father and explain the nature of God's kingdom to life-changing results: the sick were healed, the hungry were fed, the lost were found, the blind could see, the deaf hear, the lame walk, the lonely given belonging, the poor given hope, the bland and tasteless was made vibrant and delicious, the broken made whole! Original honor was restored: New Creation! When Jesus sent out his disciples to minister in His name (nature), He instructed them to embrace this same two-fold approach of grace and truth. On one hand, He said to help people experience this kind of genuine affection: "Lay hands upon them in my name." On the other hand, He instructed his followers to explain to those whose lives had been touched that, "The kingdom of God has come near you!" It was not merely a temporal, sensual "feel good" exchange. It was a spiritual happening of eternal value! Worth (honor) and wholeness were wondrously restored! And it is this same truth and grace that work miracles today, even for you and for me! As we have been called out of a dark and chaotic world back to a garden of abundance and beauty, so we are also sent back into that world to offer a new creation. To those in need, who want more, and who are willing to wrestle with God's truth and grace, we give the gospel (good news) of Jesus Christ!

That God has created us for honor is more clearly understood as we return to the beginnings of the Bible and continue in Genesis to hear the story of that first creation. It reads like a song! On each day after His handiwork, we begin learning a new chorus that is repeated at the completion of each major aspect of the known world, "It is good!" Soon we learn this refrain by heart, and it is committed to memory. There is within our hearts a melody and memory about all of God's gifts of creation, "It is good! It is good! It is good!" The blessings of God's honor and glory are spread over all His creatures. But wait! The opera is interrupted when God sees that the man He has created is without companionship and God pronounces a harsh, contrasting, temporary lyric, "It is not good for man to be alone!" So out of man's need and side, but especially out of God's compassion for mankind, God creates a companion/helpmate He calls woman. Then God changes, for emphasis, in His last verse the final chorus. On the seventh day, when God creates humankind, male and female in his own image, and places them in this garden of paradise, He sings a wonderful pronouncement, "It is very good!" And at the completion of creation (at the end of chapter 2), to emphasize the tremendous honor and glory of His creation, the scripture declares that the man and woman were with each other naked (without defensive walls, sexually honest) and there was no shame (i.e., complete glory/honor)! Much more important than any "doctrine of original sin" is this biblical description of original goodness/glory!

In many ways, it would be nice if the story ended there: a perfect Eden/ Earth of beautiful abundance where we all enjoyed loving and peaceful relationships. But that is not real, not how it is, nor how the story continues. Perhaps we could not appreciate the state of glory and honor and God's role in this gift if we did not know the painful consequences of sin and shame.

Ultimately, the Bible says that "the wages of sin is death" (opposite of creation/new life). But we do well to realize that even more than guilt, sin works to diminish and destroy life through shame. Shame is like but a little different than guilt. Guilt tells us what we did was wrong. Shame tells us that we are wrong! That we are not good! And it is this shame that alienates us from our companionship and our garden of Eden, indeed from God and the health of our soul. What began as a walk in the park turns into a lonely and stressful wilderness fight for survival. Harmony just became harm!

What began as a healthy and whole family becomes broken by sin and shame. It starts after God explains that His abundant gift of life in paradise involves an appropriate boundary. They are not to eat of the tree of knowledge of good and evil, lest they die. As a loving parent, God doesn't just say, "Don't do it just because I say so!" Wisely, God explains the natural, logical consequences of a transgression. Adam and Eve hear and understand, but fall into temptation through a dialogue with the demonic. In a revealing story about a poisonous reptile who brings toxicity by twisting the truth, this scriptural tale tells us that the couple succumbed to a disobedient choice by listening to and buying into an exaggeration of God's moral requirement. The serpent's bold lie, "I hear God says you can't eat of the fruit of any of the trees of the garden" is only partially rejected by Eve. Why? Because she buys into the white lie, "We may eat of the fruit of the trees of the Garden, but God said, 'You shall not eat of the fruit of the tree that is in the middle of the garden, nor shall you touch it, or you shall die'" (Genesis 3:2–3). The dishonesty began by becoming overly conservative. God never said, "You can't touch it!" The rebellion that followed led to believing more "half-truth" lies: "You will not die, you will be like God." False promises! Only then did the sensual seductions kick in: the fruit was beautiful and delicious. Eating this forbidden fruit even offered (sadly and ironically) to impart knowledge and wisdom. For there was indeed a price to pay: the alienation of "not good/shame"! The disobedience, blaming and shaming results in God's judgment: No more "good life" in the Garden. The snake became a symbol of evil and curse. The woman would experience pain now in having kids, yet continue to want her husband to make babies, even though he would now rule over her. For the man, his agrarian work would become laborious and not very satisfying or productive, and his end would be a return to the soil from which he was created. Dust to dust. Not good!

Just when it seems that it can't get any worse, it does. Adam and Eve in their shameful situation have a child. And in their state of dishonor, they try to overcome their shame independent from God with conceit and control as they narcissistically name their baby Cain, which sounds like the Hebrew verb, "have gotten." Their efforts though are not without God's assistance, and they have a second child, Abel, who seems to have a better attitude than his older brother. Abel grows up to shepherd sheep, while Cain follows in his dad's footsteps: he plows and plants. After they both make offerings to God, Cain discovers that while Abel's gift pleases God, Cain's gift does not. Noticing as the Lord does, that Cain's countenance had fallen from his anger, God counseled lovingly and wisely, "Why are you angry, and why has your countenance fallen? If you do well will you not be accepted? And if you do not do well, sin is lurking at the door; its desire is for you, but you must master it" (Genesis 4:6–7). But Cain's spirit of rebelliousness, resentment, and revenge prevailed. Seeking his own solution instead of God's, the sin only deepened. Cain invited Abel to go out to the field and there "rose up against him and killed his brother." This is where we get the phrase "raising Cain." And this is where a dysfunctional, shame-based family became abusive, and even more pained and alienated. Really not good!

When God questions Cain about his brother's whereabouts, he responds with another lie and liberal exaggeration of his moral responsibility, "I do not know. Am I my brother's keeper?" Because the word "keeper" was one used for tending animals such as pigs or sheep, the obvious answer to Cain's question was, "No, you are not your brother's keeper. But you are your brother's brother!" I can imagine God saying that in sad/mad frustration. Exaggeration, whether liberal or conservative, are easier to reject.

We now hear that though there would be further consequences of hurt and separation as Cain finds himself a fearful, wandering fugitive, God does not abandon or quit caring and even promises providential protection to Cain. One of Cain's descendants, Jubal, mercifully becomes the ancestor of those who play wind or stringed musical instruments (where we get our word jubilation)! Remembering him and God's gift to music, we honor our spiritual mothers and fathers and, as always, God's amazing grace.

But then, guess what happens? A more spiritually mature Adam and Eve move forward and have a third child and humbly name the new son "Seth"! His name resembles the Hebrew verb appointed, and Eve gratefully exclaims, "God has appointed for me another child instead of Abel, because Cain killed him" (Genesis 4:25b). It seems that they had come to realize that a child is not a proud possession that we as parents produce on our own and simply pressure to do our will, but a gift from God to celebrate and nurture in His likeness, a sign that God has not given up on the world or its families!

As we think of healthier, happier families and a sign from God about His desire for that to be the norm, I remember then the rainbow and the commitment from God to work at achieving that, though not with destructive removals like the Great Flood, but through more gracious strategies. After trying this with Noah and his family with less than excellent results, God tried another approach. After years and generations went by, God chose another family to bless in order to bring blessings to all families. It was the improbable family of Abraham and Sarah.

Abraham (father of many) had been Abram (high father), while Sarah (lady or princess) had been Sarai (contentious). Through their faithfulness, God would reckon their lives as righteous or honorable, even though their attitudes and actions were still a work in progress. In their old age, God granted them a son (whose name meant laughter, Isaac), who turned a skeptical chuckle into an expression of grateful joy! In a difficult and often deceiving world (and extended family), Isaac's son, Jacob (supplanter)/Israel (one who wrestles with god), goes through a long and difficult process of producing a child of honor, Joseph. His name means "he will add," and his even more difficult and demeaning journey would amazingly add honor to himself and his family of choice (wife and children) and, in another sense, to the people of Egypt and Israel and also to his family of origin and future descendants. Through faithful (wise and brave) decisions, Joseph would overcome the shame of his victimization to enjoy the honor/glory of victorious living. He went from victim to victor! The meaning of his family's names also indicates this point in their dramatic story. Joseph's wife, Asenath's name means "she belongs to her father," indicating a faithful woman. His son's name, Manassah, means "make to forget," expressing how he was part of Joseph's healthy grieving process in forgiveness. His other son, Ephraim, whose name means "to be fruitful" claims the home harvest blessings of an honorable life. Joseph lived to enjoy his grandchildren and great-grandchildren by both sons (it would be very nice if I/we all could).

It would also be nice to say, "And they all lived happily ever after." But of course the story goes on (in Exodus) to say, "Now a new king arose over Egypt who did not know Joseph." Suspicion and selfishness led to persecution and slavery. The Egyptians became "ruthless" (without loyalty), and sin expressed itself in racial, economic, cultural, and political ways. And in their darkest hour, the one God of Creation, began working out a new chapter, a "way out" (meaning of Exodus). His spirit and word would again bring deliverance from the dark chaos and deep waters. Moses, whose name means "drawn out," became God's chosen messenger and leader to liberate his chosen people, drawing them out of their slavery in Egypt.

Without going into the whole story of this exciting and miraculous escape adventure, a key to them/us becoming a free people of blessing was God's gift of a covenant code we call the Ten Commandments. Through it, God provided a set of guidelines for right living by honoring God and one another. In the twentieth chapter of Exodus (way out) we hear God declare himself to be a God of liberation/freedom. God reminds the descendants of Abraham, Isaac, and Jacob that He is their God who has delivered them from slavery. This, God's identity/activity, is the preface and foundation of the ten covenant guidelines He is about to give them, all of which are important to commit to memory and heart and action. As Christians and as Aggies, we are called to a higher order of commitment to the honor habit: in heads and hearts and hands and homes, indeed our whole earthly home.

God calls/commands His children/people to a covenant relationship by honoring Him in our lives in ten major ways:

1. By putting God first; claiming Him as our ultimate concern: making His honor our top priority in all we think, feel, and do.
2. By not making or accepting any phony substitutes for God (e.g., property, popularity, pleasures/pleasantries, or power over, etc.)
3. By not dishonoring God's name with misuse: mockery, sarcasm, silliness, etc. God's name is His nature, which is steadfast, liberating, prospering love. Greater love!
4. By remembering and keeping the Sabbath holy through regular rituals of rest, recreation, and renewal; for family inspiration and instruction; for shared worship and witness. By honoring God's weekly rhythm of restoration and redemption.
5. By honoring our "parents" and other family members. Included here should be other contributing "forefathers and foremothers."
6. By respecting/honoring others' health/well-being/lives. All lives matter!
7. By respecting/honoring others' sexual integrity.
8. By respecting/honoring others' property
9. By respecting/honoring others' reputation.
10. By respecting/honoring others through our thoughts, desires, and plans.

God concluded these commandments with a display of his might (his own version of "shock and awe") to help motivate His people to not sin. The scriptures note that the "fear of the Lord is the beginning of wisdom." Aggies and Christians need to accept accountability: that there are consequences for our choices. As an active member of my church's youth group, I have always remembered a counselor's wisdom: "We are free to make choices, but we are not free to choose (avoid/change) the consequences." Interestingly, it is in the second commandment that this truth is emphasized and explained. In it, God declares that iniquity/idolatry will result in sad consequences that will be shared and suffered by the family, being visited upon not only the children, but even by their children and their children's children. Boy, is that motivation to try and get it right! As a matter of fact, I thought at first that this seemed too harsh, though in studying family systems theory, I believe it is realistic. But what I realized upon further examination was not the harshness, but the hopefulness and graciousness of this commandment. For it is the first commandment with a promise: that God's steadfast love will bless our faithfulness to the thousandth generation! Even more motivation to love God and keep his commandments!

This new code of conduct/honor was good and helped God's people prosper, but as time went by proved to be insufficient. Through a later prophet, Jeremiah, God foretold a "new and improved" covenant. It would be a shift from law to love, a heartfelt spiritual experience of God's grace expressed as mercy or forgiveness. In Jeremiah 31:31–34, the Lord announces a more mature approach to righteousness (or right relationship between God and His people), which is God's greatest desire and our greatest goal or purpose in life. God's blessing of honor would transcend people's performance and certainly the performance of their parents or grandparents* (Jer.31:27–30). "I will be their God, and they shall be my people" (Jer. 31:33b).

As Christians, we believe that it was Jesus Christ who delivered this new covenant and the gift of abundant, joyful, and eternal life! By grace through faith in Him, we are saved from our bondage to sin, shame, and death! That by trusting and following Him, we have a way out of the human dilemma of our slavery to iniquity and its consequences to ourselves, our families, and to many others in the society. Jesus has simplified and focused the law of the Old Testament with a new commandment, "Love one another (as he has loved us.)" We honor God by caring for one another. It does not do away with the other commandments, but fulfills them. In John's Gospel, he explains that it is by this love for one another that it can be told/noticed that we are Christians. At the end of Matthew's Gospel, Christ describes this to be the difference during the final judgment, that as we care for even "the least of these who are members of my family"* (Mt. 25:40), we have cared for (and honored) him. And there will ultimately be for our choices eternal consequences, of blessing or curse, "bliss or blister"!

As Aggies, we are also invited to learn through the many traditions of Aggieland, to be there for others in a caring way that brings honor to them, ourselves, our school, and our society. As Christians, we are challenged in the New Testament, "Let love be genuine; hate what is evil, hold fast to what is good; love one another with mutual affection; outdo one another in showing honor. Do not lag in zeal, be ardent in spirit, serve the Lord. Rejoice in hope, be patient in suffering, persevere in prayer. Contribute to the needs of the saints; extend hospitality to strangers" (Romans 12:9–13). Or put more simply in the First Letter of Peter 2:17a, "Honor everyone."

Notes

Chapter 2

Suggested Study/Reflection/Discussion Questions

1. In my description of Lawrence Sullivan Ross, I used the words courage, compassion, integrity, and faith. Do you agree and why? What words would you add to describe his honor?

2. Honor is not only a noun, but also a verb. Ross Volunteers, for example, are chosen as examples of the noun and with the function of the verb. Can you explain? What is the connection or relationship of the noun "honor" to the verb "honor"? (Hint: Respecting others is the path to respectability.)

3. What are some of the ways that you honor others? (1 Peter 2:17 says, "Honor everyone!) Parents? Other family members? Persons in authority? Persons under your authority? Friends? Strangers? Aggies? Others? How does your own sense of honor and self-esteem affect your ability to honor others (or conversely shame others with criticism, sarcasm, and condemnation because of low self-esteem)? How is truth and grace through faith the answer?

4. How does one's commitment to the ethical code to "not lie, cheat, or steal" honor others? How does Jesus make sense of this ethic with the Golden Rule, "Do unto others as you would have others do unto you"?

5. Why not tolerate the dishonesty of others who "lie, cheat, or steal"?

6. In the Bible's story of creation, how is "spirit" connected to "glory"? (Hint: glory is symbolized by light shining forth. This is God's first act of creation.)

7. People's hunger for honor and glory is so strong that they are sometimes tempted to lie, cheat, and steal in order to obtain honor and glory! Explain. How does this inevitably work out? Can you name examples or illustrations (e.g., Lance Armstrong)?

8. When honor has been lost to shame, how does "in Christ there is new creation" describe the process called "redemption"? Why is "grace" truly "amazing"?

9. Community/healthy family is connected to honor/worth in the creation story when God says it is "not good" to be alone and "very good" to be together! How does belonging to the Aggie community/family brings a sense of honor/goodness?

10. Name some ways that shame (attitude of "We don't matter.") brings death (e.g., abuse, addictions, failure through fear, depression, etc.)?

11. Someone said, "Grandchildren are God's way of blessing you for not killing your children!" Why was "Seth" such a great name for our first grandchild?

12. Can you tell others your family story? Your biblical family story of the Patriarchs? How do the meanings of the names add to the story?

13. How are the Ten Commandments and the Aggie Code of Honor ideal ethical guides? How are they similar? Different? Do you have a "guiding star"? How would you describe it/him?

14. The second commandment promises us that our faithfulness will bless our children and their children to the thousandth generation! Does this realization stir thankfulness within you for all the contributions of your ancestors? Motivate your faithfulness in your family to descendants?

15. How does the New Covenant transcend the Old Covenant? What is the New Covenant? How are choice and consequence connected?

16. What are some ways you would like to be more honoring? In Saint Peter's letter in the New Testament, he said, "Honor everyone." Who are some that are hungry for honor? That you have neglected? That are high priority?

17. How do Christians and Aggies belong to a "mutual admiration society"? (See YouTube, Teresa Brewer's "Mutual Admiration Society," 1956, written by Harold Karr and Matt Dubey.)

Former players of the 2011 NCAA National WBB Championship Team: (l-r) Sydney Carter (WNBA), Mary Ann Baker (assistant Miss. St,), and Sydney Coulson, newly hired assistant with the Aggies. Reunited for a game in 2014, with Miss. St. U. Former Students are encouraged to remain 12th Men and alway an important part of the Aggie teams. Our Howdy/hospitality is forever!

Danielle Adams

Some of the WBK team I enjoyed supporting as a volunteer chaplain, a Twelfth Man and a senior Yell Leader includes Fighting Texas Aggies: Adaora Elonu, Kelsey "Kickin'" Assarian, Demetria Buchanan (whose dad also "preached"), Sydney Colson, Sydney Carter, (Energy= Sydney C²), and Danielle (God is Judge) Adams (National Champion MVP).

Sydney Carter and Sydney Colson

Demetria Buchanan   *Adaora Elonu*

Sydney Colson

Kelsey "Kickin'" Assarian

I have enjoyed being supportive of WBB coaches Gary Blair (Hall of Fame and Aggie Vic Schaeffer (assistant, defensive coordinator) (see "Practicing Powerful Prayer" in Appendices). (Note ATM necktie from Coach Blair.

Our first "two in one year' to the WNBA, graduates Aquonesia Franklin and Morenike Atunrace. After attending their games in December 2004 and eating with them as wide-eyed freshmen at their table for a luncheon, I decided to support them and their team as a "volunteer chaplain". Here we celebrate their return to Aggieland.

Celebrating a very special 2012 "Heisman" football season with former classmate (late sixties Mechanical Engineering) and now former A&M President R. Bowen Loftin.

CHAPTER 3

CHRISTIAN HOSPITALITY & "HOWDY!"

Getting to know our waitress one evening as Donna and I dined out on our date night, this A&M student said she loved it here. I remember asking this out-of-state Aggie why she loved being here in Aggieland. What was it that made Bryan College Station such a great place to live? Above all the wonderful places to eat, things to see and do, and quality services and resources of all sorts, she immediately said, "The people here are what makes it great! The people here tend to be friendly, honest, respectful, and caring. They are not snobbish, but down to earth and fun to be around!" I agreed with her.

One of my most pleasant experiences as a pastor for about thirty years in Texas was doing Aggie weddings. They were "close encounters" of the best kind! Beyond the honesty and cooperation from the couples during the premarital counseling (which was always satisfying helping them "tie the knot" more securely), Aggies in general would combine respect with recreation. They knew how to have a good time and still be responsible. At the ceremony and celebration afterward, they were both faithful and fun!

And I believe that the quality of character of people that we enjoy in the Aggie family begins with the values incorporated in our family traditions. It is learned by understanding them, embracing them, and living them better. That is primarily why I am writing this book. I trust that at the heart of most Aggie traditions is their time-tested ability to train Aggies to be better persons, that is, to help them develop and hone habits for highly effective living. These long-lived rituals nurture beliefs and behaviors that have served Aggies well for many generations. They help instill foundational ideals and shape sound character. They result in a culture of courtesy and encouragement, of challenges and championships! Most of these traditions are built on the basic values of the first two chapters: greater love and honor. The more intentionally we can understand these traditions, the more we can live them. An old joke asks, "What is the most important vitamin for a Christian?" The answer: B1 (i.e. be one). Avoid hypocrisy: walk the talk. This answer is also true for Aggies. It is certainly true of the important Christian value of hospitality and the Aggie tradition of "Howdy!"

As a freshman (fish) in Company F-1, I remember one of the first traditions I was taught was that of "Howdy!" Our outfit motto was "F-1, Finest First" ("the best damn outfit on campus!"), which, as most traditions do, helped to instill pride and unity. And learning the "Howdy!" tradition of greeting others was not only the first, but one of the finest traditions at Texas A&M. Like many worthwhile things, it was not easy as a new student. For, in addition to saying "Howdy!" to others, we were supposed to remember and speak the person's name as well. And if we did not know or remember their name, we were to meet them until we did. This traditional ritual was called "whipping out." We would whip out our right hand, and as we firmly shook hands, tell the other person our name. After they told us their name, we would say that we were glad to meet them, and ask where they were from. This exchange would continue as we were also to inquire as to their major and share ours.

Now you can imagine the challenge of learning this discipline, especially as you were sometimes tested by upperclassmen to see if you were really listening and remembering! As days and weeks went by, additional degrees of difficulty were sometimes added by changing step (for we were to keep in step with the person we were meeting) as we walked. Also challenging was the meeting of the friends of the upperclassman. I remember one particularly fired-up sophomore who after a midweek yell practice introduced himself as "King Kong from Hong Kong, majoring in Ping Pong!" I of course could not laugh or even smile as it was not a fish's privilege to show emotions. By Thanksgiving, we were to have learned the names of all the cadets in our dormitory. A common fish nightmare was getting taken into and caught in another dorm, especially the Band dorm. You could spend what seemed like eternity trapped there! Fish would avoid even going to the restrooms to escape having to speak to everyone in the hallway of their own dorm, much less another's dorm!

But more than imagining the difficulty of this ritual of greeting, I would like you to envision the benefits of the "Howdy!" tradition. For a quality of greeting sets the tone of a whole community. This basic courtesy raises the quality of community as it strengthens an atmosphere of respectful relationships. "Howdy!" is something of a folksy combination of "Hi!" and "How do you do?" or "How are you?" "Howdy!" says to each Aggie and visitor to campus that he/she is important and cared about; valued and noticed; honored and loved. This deepest of human needs begins to be met as we take the time, energy, and bother to offer a friendly greeting that communicates, "You matter. I care about how you are doing. I'd like to know you better. You are interesting. And I wish you well." And the person practicing this habit learns to have the courage and confidence to reach out to others; to have the compassion to express friendliness; and the honor not to take others for granted. Of course in the beginning of performing this duty, there may be more focus on simply saying the right words. But in time, those involved become more familiar and comfortable with the routine and can be more focused on the person(s) being greeted.

In advancing the strength of relationships and building the sense of self-worth of the Aggie family, as well as those outside this community whom we serve, we do well to understand the ingredients in the recipe of good greeting and healthy hospitality. Biblically, we are commanded in five different places in the epistles of the New Testament to "Greet one another with a holy kiss." Words of welcome were important, but not enough. Signs of affectionate but appropriate touch were to accompany this greeting. The word holy, which means "special" or "set apart," refers to avoiding the hurtful ways of a sinful world where touch is too often violent and abusive, mean or molesting (disrespectfully exploitive or invasive). Holy means caring and respectful, gentle, tender, and with sincere affection. Holy kiss means mutually consensual affection. For a negative example, Judas's betrayal kiss on Jesus's cheek was not a holy kiss! In the Mediterranean areas in which our biblical faith began and grew, there continues the literal practice of a kiss on one or both cheeks of the persons greeting one another. The large Sicilian-American population in Bryan, into which I married, still practices this ritual to various degrees. In American culture, the handshake is the most commonly accepted approach. The handshake of Aggies is expected to be firm and friendly, assertive and accommodating. That does not mean a handshake that is hard and hurtful! For years, folks have experimented with other expressions such as high fives, hugs, fist bumps, and even chest bumps, depending on the setting. A score on the football field for example is often greeted with a chest bump by the players involved, a passionate kiss of one's date or spouse, and high fives with the other fans around us. In a way it is a greeting of God's glory, His power at work among us, celebrating a manifestation of His victorious life incarnate (spirit become flesh) in the community of believers. The game becomes, in a sense, an act of worship, a celebration of the mysterious and amazing Spirit of Greater Love powerfully among us!

And as these rituals recognize this "glory" coming into our presence, they also pay respect upon the parting of persons. For example, we (holy) hug and bless with words when we say goodbye, "So good to see you, _____(name). Take care. Good luck with . . . Have a great . . ." and a wave as we leave our loved ones. Goodbye means literally "God be with you (and bless you while we are parted)." A quality farewell greeting is as important as the introductory greeting.

As a way to recognize and honor those of rank or distinguished service in the armed forces, the most common tradition is the salute. Its origins are a sign of respect to the "glory" or "God's shining" from the person being greeted by shielding our eyes from their brightness. Similarly, this is what originally was being communicated when we tipped our hat to a lady! These are still wonderful ways to communicate, "You are special, awesome, amazing, fabulous, etc., you shine and I honor you!"

With our immediate family, we also move toward an ideal of love and trust as we express affection when we come together and when we leave each other's presence. That includes greetings in the morning that say, "Good morning _____ (name). How are you?" or "How are you feeling? How did you sleep?" and a cuddle in bed or a holy hug or kiss, or in the case of my sons when they were younger, a back rub, hand touch, or fist bump. These greetings are truly a way to show hospitality to God's presence, for Jesus promised, "Where two or more are gathered in my name, there am I also." At the supper table, our family held hands as we shared a prayer. Our tradition was for each person to say, "Thank you God for . . . (at least one thing), and/or "Help us God with . . . (some issue of need)." We would conclude with a "Wesleyan Grace" (usually sung): "Be present at our table Lord, be here and everywhere adored. These favors bless and grant that we may feast in fellowship with Thee. Amen." This was of course helpful in giving us hints for further dinner conversation. For example, instead of the tempting response "Nothing." to "What did you do today?" their mother and I usually had some good indicators in celebrating what had gone well with our kids and expressing concern for what had been painful or a problem. Greeting traditions help set an atmosphere of trust where we/others are encouraged and are more open and directed to further encouragement and guidance.

Likewise, at bedtime, we tried to maintain the tradition of saying good night with a back rub, a short bedtime story, a tuck under the covers, a short prayer (see Appendix Champion Children of God Songbook), and a good night (holy)kiss (usually on the forehead). Also, if there was a major concern, it was a good time for a little conversation. Although we have led busy lives, our sons and we as parents never regretted taking some time for this "quality time." Like the "Howdy!" tradition, this discipline took time, patience, and perseverance to learn and establish. Again, God's greater love and honor were the foundational values that undergirded all forms of hospitality. But it was these treasured traditions that became holy habits and that helped "blessings flow" and happen for all of us and others through us!

A tradition that is not practiced is obviously not very helpful, except that it is reexamined and reevaluated, and perhaps revised and reinstituted in light of our contemporary obstacles and opportunities. Our oldest son, Jason, was born an hour before the Fourth of July, and, I noted, has been an independent person ever since! After his junior year in high school, he was offered a scholarship to and participated in the prestigious Young Scholars program that summer at the campus of the University of Texas in Austin doing biomedical research, running experiments on the refreshment of athletes. We were shocked to hear him say that he was considering doing his undergraduate work there as well! I did not pressure him to go to Texas A&M, but asked him to compare the two campuses: the atmospheres of the two revealed by the body language, attire, and conversations of the students. Which student body was friendlier, more respectful, more honest, more passionate and compassionate, etc.? The differences were quite obvious, and Jason independently chose to come to Aggieland. And I believe the "Howdy!" tradition helped make that difference!

Many times have I heard students, student athletes, and former students say that it was the atmosphere of hospitality that convinced them that Texas A&M is where they wanted to come to school. They would say it felt like home or family! And a great many of these went on to become outstanding contributors to Aggieland, whether academically or athletically or simply by their character and leadership, both while they attended classes here and/or after they graduated. Throughout many generations of Aggies, we Aggies have made a difference and gained a reputation that began simply with the tradition of a warm and genuine hospitality that goes by the name of "Howdy!" It is indeed simple yet profound!

But for some time, that tried and true tradition has come under the assault of such obstacles as cell phones, iPods, earphones, headphones, laptops, smart-phones, etc. Technological changes have come at an increasingly rapid and unexpected speed and require creative legislation, such as "no-texting zones" to maintain safety and well-being. As recently as 1943, Thomas Watson, chairman of IBM said, "I think there is a world market for maybe five computers." Even more recently, in 1977, Ken Olsen, president, chairman, and founder of Digital Equipment Corporation said, "There is no reason anyone would want a computer in their home." Albert Einstein, who did more scientifically than perhaps anyone to pioneer and spark the technological boom of the last one hundred years and who died in 1955 (when I was in first grade), noted, "The significant problems we face cannot be solved at the same level of thinking we were at when we created them" and "It has become appallingly obvious that our technology has exceeded our humanity." Even as far back as the mid-1800s, Henry David Thoreau observed, "Men have become the tools of their tools." Personally, I celebrate the transparency enabled by the computer/Internet age where it is not so easy for evil to be disguised or good suppressed or truth denied. Even as I have been writing this book, there have been revolutionary movements around the world attributed to the uncovering of corruption and abusive power through the aid of this information/communication superhighway! A little light can overcome a lot of darkness. The "Information Age" offers a world of wealth in images and ideas. It is of course up to us how we use them. President Dwight D. Eisenhower warned in his inaugural address on January 20, 1953, "A people that values its privileges above its principles soon loses both." Though first spoken at different points in history, I believe these quotes apply today. The comedian Steven Wright quipped, "I have an existential map; it has 'You are here' written all over it."

Certainly, the blame for an erosion of character and wise values is not only on technology. We seem to have an increasing depersonalization of society in general. And with the decades, there also seems to be an increasing decadence. Larger cities, bigger schools, homogenized suburbs, mass media, and mass marketing have each chipped away at the foundations of relational trust, respect, and responsibility. Absolute truth, justice, and morality have been questioned, assaulted, and relativized. The commercialization of a culture changes community into commodity. Persons become viewed as property or pawns, leaving many feeling used and abused, deflected, and neglected.

Addressing both our school and our churches, our workplaces, and marketplaces, I would warn here each about neglecting our heritage of hospitality. Though none of us are perfect, it is important to remember that our actions represent more than ourselves. As Christians/church members, we are ambassadors of Christ. Do others meet the truth and grace of Christ in you? When others see you wearing an Aggie ring, shirt, or cap, do they gain an impression of someone with loyalty and honor? And as an Aggie, when you are driving your car, do you practice responsibility and respect and graciousness and courtesy? Do you show honor and respect as well as safety by using your blinker? Others see our Aggie decals, and whether we like it or not, our driving conduct makes an impression, good or bad. Perhaps at sporting events, as much as anywhere, although we stand by our teams as Twelfth Men and do our best to BTHO our opponents, we do well to remember that their followers and supporters are our guests on campus. Even if they tend to be rude and obnoxious, we should not lower ourselves to their discourtesy. "Do not overcome evil with evil, but overcome evil with good" (Romans 12:21). I admit, vengeance can be very tempting, but God promises to take care of that!

Jesus's anger and indignation is greatest in the gospel stories when he observes this dishonor to God as we devalue persons. He seeks to confront and reform it and "cleanse the temple" by refusing to tolerate the moneychangers' ways. His zeal is kindled when he recognizes that what was intended to be a family setting of hospitality (spiritually holy communication: "My Father's house," a "house of prayer") has become a commercial enterprise of dishonest self-interest and greed ("a house of market" and a "den of thieves")! As Christians and as Aggies, we should regularly examine ourselves, our churches, and our school to see where we are on this spectrum. There is perhaps an appropriate time and place for a market mentality. As a pastor in deep south Texas, I heard on TV a store advertise, "Mucho mas por mucho menos!" meaning "much more for much less." This attitude may help us be more effective shoppers, buyers, and consumers. But when we bring this attitude into our relationships with those we are supposed to love and treat as family, seeking to "get as much as we can for as little as we can," it turns us into robbers instead of relatives. This is the temptation of idolatry, to bow to mammon and worship the "almighty dollar," to descend into greed and graft. Wealth is a terrific servant, but a terrible master. And Jesus explained (Mt.25:40) that whatever we have done or not done to even the least of His brothers and sisters, we have done to Him. The church family and the Aggie family would do best to always remember this and demonstrate sincere hospitality, generosity, and friendship.

We share as Christians and Aggies this tremendous tradition of friendly greeting and meeting of others. Let us strive to live it faithfully, wisely, and joyously! In doing so, we bring glory to God and love and honor to our school, others, and ourselves.

"Let love be genuine; hate what is evil, hold fast to what is good; love one another with mutual affection; outdo one another in showing honor" (Romans 12:9–10). And, "May the God of steadfastness and encouragement grant you to live in harmony with one another, in accordance with Christ Jesus, so that together you may with one voice glorify the God and Father of our Lord Jesus Christ. Welcome one another, therefore, just as Christ has welcomed you, for the glory of God" (Romans 15:7).

Notes

Chapter 3

Questions for Study, Reflection, and Discussion

1. "Howdy!" is about greeting and getting to know others, and establishing friendships. From "Never talk to strangers" recluse to "Never met a stranger" extrovert, on a scale of 1 to 10, where do you and your family members usually stand?

2. What aspects of hospitality most challenge you?

3. It is said that we don't get a second chance to make a good first impression. Are you comfortable with a firm handshake, an assertive yet friendly tone of voice, good eye contact, a winning smile, confident posture, focused interest in the person you are meeting, the use of words of affirmation and bridling of disrespectful communication, etc. If not will you practice the effectiveness of your "Howdy!" hospitality?

4. God in the culture of Israel is often called, "The Lord of Hosts", indicating their value of hospitality. The entertainment of guests was a sacred duty. I personally empathized with the discomfort of these newcomers and sought to give them special attention. Who in your life is in need of this hospitality?

5. Our oldest son Jason sponsored/hosted "transfer students" at T-Camp. How can you improve the welcome of these newcomers? International students? Non-Christians: Jews, Muslims, agnostics, atheists, others?

6. In Hebrews 13:2 we are instructed to offer hospitality to strangers with the hopeful feeling that we may be "entertaining angels without knowing it!" Think of (and share) a surprise blessing from someone you met and befriended.

7. The Venn Diagram invented by in is a mathematical symbol of what two or more entities have in common. In the "Greater Love" logo (on the book cover) this Venn device also forms a fish, an early symbol of Christ from the Greek acronym Ichthus: Jesus Christ God's Son and Savior. It was a less dangerous way to meet and declare one's discipleship to Christ. It points to a core value of a hospitality which is also careful, seeking to find common ground and connect. What

does this mean? How does this apply to "Howdy!" and "whipping out?" How does this seeking of mutuality help make us better "partners in purpose"? Brothers/sisters in Christ, etc.?

8. How does hospitality emerge as a core value from honor and respect, and move us toward the core values of loyalty and unity? Excellence? Integrity? Leadership? Unselfish service?

9. How do these all spring from "Greater Love"?

10. How does it all begin then with God's hospitality to us? (Hint: While we were still sinners, Christ died for us! [Romans 5:8])

11. Pope Francis is the first Jesuit Papal leader of the Roman Catholic Church. How has his emphasis on Christian hospitality in the style/ teaching of Jesus brought refreshment and energy to Christ's Church, the body of all His followers?

12. What are some goals of hospitality that you would like to adopt? (For example: inviting newcomers to ....) Try making eye contact, using the persons name, and really listening after asking, "How are you?" Try empathizing (hearing the feelings) and paraphrasing. Try smiling. Offer to pray and help.

*We love to have Aggie/
Christian fellowship
on our recently
refurbished deck.
Backyard Barbecues
like tailgates are a
great tradition!*

*My best cheerleader
(12th Man) growing up
was my mother, Maybeth
Barry Bauerschlag. Here
after I was awarded the
Outstanding Freshman
(Best Drilled) medal for
'66-'67 Company F-1.*

*Mother's Day with my
then financeé Donna and
present 12th Man/wife.*

Some of our amazing 2012-13 freshmen: Jordan Jones, Courtney Williams, Curtyce Knox, and Rachel Mitchell.

Celebrating another great season at Women's Basketball Banquet 2013 with Karla Gilbert (Assistant Head Coach Kelly Bonds in the background).

Senior 2012-2013 veteran forward Kristi Bellock played a key role in the Women's Basketball teams success.

The Aggie Dance Team brings cheer/energy to sports events at Reed Arena, primarily to Aggie Basketball games. These officers, led by Captain Brooke, on the right offered to take this photo after a WBB victory. I discovered/met Brooke's dad who was also a C.O. and RV in the 70s

The Twelfth Man Tradition began with a multi-sport support experience! Here Derel Walker, Mike Evans, and Tra Carson enjoy Aggie basketball and a half-time photo. Travis Labhart was to the right of Tra, but didn't get into the photo!

Joyful appreciation which honors and encourages the faithful hard work and loyal dedication of our athletes is the foundation of effective support. Here, after midnight, the Twelfth Man welcomed home the first year SEC Women's Basketball Tournament Champions with Head Coach Gary Blair holding the microphone.

CHAPTER 4

CHRISTIAN FRIENDSHIP &
THE TWELFTH MAN

"The Twelfth Man" Song

Texas Aggies down in Aggieland
We've got Aggie Spirit to a man
Stand united, that's the Aggie theme
We're the Twelfth Man on the team

B efore national championships in college football were formally declared, the Fightin' Texas Aggie football team played a historic game on January 2, 1922, against Centre College, then the top ranked team in the nation. When the available players on the team were becoming depleted due to injuries, Coach D. X. Bible remembered a two-sport student player already active on the basketball team who had not suited up for the bowl game. Coach Bible called E. King Gill from the stands. The student came down, put on a football uniform, and stood by, ready to come in and play as needed for the remainder of the hard-fought game. A&M won 22–14. And though the coach and his team did not need to send him onto the field, his readiness to serve and sacrifice for his school became a historic symbol of the tradition of greater love known to Aggies and many around the world as the Twelfth Man. This spirit of unselfish support and readiness to help others in their struggles has been an inspiration throughout the decades and generations of Aggies since.

The devotion that Aggies feel for their school is displayed to their teams and fellow students with enthusiasm and commitment. The Twelfth Man tradition is embraced by students standing during our team's play and giving loud encouragement to our athletes. This includes both traditional, learned "yells" and spontaneous cheering. Engaging the opponents in good natured/good sportsmanship verbal harassment can also be part of the Twelfth Man's support. Good judgment here should wisely be used with discretion to avoid unsportsmanlike conduct. Frequent yell practices (what other schools call "pep rallies") help ensure that students are familiar with the yells and are fired up to give emotional support to the Aggie teams playing. Five yell leaders, three senior and two juniors, are elected by the student body to provide student-based leadership, another important Aggie tradition. They will choose the appropriate yell or song at the appropriate time, giving the traditional sign for it, and then leading the Twelfth Man through it. As such, the yell leaders are a catalyst for crowd enthusiasm. Aggies don't wait for their teams to get them excited; they understand that their role is the duty of further firing up the team. So they initiate yells and look for opportunities/situations to bring encouragement. Signs of minor success are celebrated and offered strong support toward major success! The Twelfth Man promotes momentum. Minor failures are accompanied with assurances of continued support and encouragement. Major criticism leads to major discouragement and failure and is itself a failure in effective leadership. Detractor two-percenters diminish momentum. Wet blankets can put fires out! True Aggies are all Twelfth Men and learn the importance of yelling for the team instead of (like most other schools and some "two percenters") mainly yelling at them. Athletes at A&M are seen as an important part of our community and not just as a commodity. They are valued as persons, not property or pawns; family, not fodder; friends, not slaves. While group goals have priority over individual ones, respect and honor for each person are valued and maintained. To just expect superiority is kin to an attitude of entitlement, and as such is an enemy of success, and a failure of loyalty. This is good Christian ethics and good Aggie ethics. Encouragement means "lift", not "push"!

The Christian basis of being this kind of loyal, supportive friend are found in many places in the scriptures, songs, and other traditions of the Christian faith. The beginnings of God's plan for a king and a Messiah or Christ (eternal, ultimate king) started with Ruth, a Moabitess woman who expressed her loyal love for her Jewish mother-in-law Naomi by refusing to abandon her at a very difficult time. "Do not press me to leave you or to turn back from following you! Where you go I will go; Where you lodge, I will lodge; your people will be my people, and your God my God. Where you die I will die—there will I be buried. May the Lord do thus and so to me, and more as well, if even death parts me from you!" (Ruth 1:16).

God redeemed this shamed (Moabites were known as a shamefully incestuous tribe) widow (whose name Ruth means "friend") with gracious glory and reversed the loss of her first husband with her new husband Boaz (whose name means "swiftness"; he was a kinsman of Naomi's), and give eventually obvious victorious living! She had become heir to God's promise and plan of blessing to Abraham through her faithfulness/loyal love or righteousness. Hers was a commitment/covenant to God's greater love. God's promise (in the second of the Ten Commandments) to bless children for the faithfulness of their parents to the thousandth generation was realized in her great-grandson, David, a humble shepherd boy, who would become one of Israel's greatest kings! And eventually, David's descendant, Jesus of Nazareth, would turn out to be the Good Shepherd/King of Kings, the Messiah, the Son of God, and Savior of the world! In him, we enjoy the salvation of a new creation! His mother, Mary, exhibited this same spirit of Ruth as she responded to God's plan to have her bear His child by the power of the Holy Spirit. Though still an engaged virgin, she replied in faith, "Let it be" ("with me according to your word")! God's greater love indeed often shows itself as an awesome mystery/magic we call miracles!

Jesus perfected this loyal, greater love and showed it through many acts of healing and redemption. Then he demonstrated it decisively on the cross and from an empty tomb! His redemptive witness is communicated most clearly in the Gospel of John. Not only did he teach us to "love one another as I have loved you," but he even gave us a new name, "Friend" (Ruth). He said, "I do not call you servants (slaves) any longer . . . I have called you 'friends'" (John 15:15 portions). Indeed, in the other books/letters of the New Testament we are also called family, honored brothers and sisters of Christ, adopted through faith as royal children of the divine king of the universe. In John 14, we hear Jesus comfort all of His disciples (those who follow him) with the support of the Holy Spirit, which he calls the paraclete, translated variously as "advocate" or "counselor" or "comforter," and meaning literally "one called to your side." That sounds a lot like the historical, spiritual roots of the Twelfth Man! The Twelfth Man is one called out to be there for support, to stand by our side with encouragement, to watch our backs for adversaries, and to help us fight our battles in the good fight, to be a bearer of the (Holy) Spirit!

Whether as Aggies or Christians, to accept this call and choose to embrace the value of loyal love is to be filled with the spirit of "Ruth/friend/ family." In accepting this choice, God fills our hearts with the fire of His truth and grace, the power of His glory, and the joy of victorious living. God cleanses us as we repent and renounce the dark spirits of idolatry, the spirit of ruthlessness, of fear and slavery of selfishness and greed, of deception and sin. And in faith we receive the gift of life: new and eternal, joyful and abundant, now and always. God forgives our foolish, selfish errancy and restores to us the honor of His image and righteousness. God's greater love redeems our lives from shame to shalom (peace and wholeness) and reverses the postcreation curse from humiliation to honor! Now we celebrate our new identities as royal family and friend! From alpha to omega, from beginning to end, He is our Lord and Savior, and we are His! Thus, also the flaming heart filled with Christ's Greater Love logo of Home Harvest Ministries of Aggieland and of this Greater Love book.

As I recently watched the Winter Olympics, I was impressed by the sacrifices of so many parents of the athletes from all over the world so that their children could enjoy the glory of fulfilling their talents and abilities. Their sacrifices were only exceeded by their joy at seeing their sons or daughters potential being realized and honored. Then it occurred to me that this is like what God (our heavenly parent) has done through the sacrificial gift of His son, Jesus Christ, and the joy God feels as we embrace His truth and grace! We are redeemed for God's glory, embodying God's power for victorious living! God greatly enjoys lifting us to championship status! In other words, if God had a wallet, our picture would be in it; if He had a refrigerator, our photo (and/or team photo) would be on it! Because God loves us so much, He delights in our success! Just as a mom or dad is overjoyed when he or she experiences their child performing or competing well, so even more is God blessed and glorified in the same way, for God is our loving and proud heavenly parent.

This again is the same joy and honor that we share as an Aggie Twelfth Man living out this rich tradition. To encourage another to do well is to share their success. To be a Twelfth Man is to actually be a player on the team and therefore rightly enjoy being a part of their play, their struggles and their championship trophies, medals, and honors. For to support others in their success is to nurture our own self-esteem, success, and victorious status. Jesus taught His followers that as we give to others we receive ourselves. It is the opposite of our commercialized, consumer/capitalist market place mentality where people try to "get as much as they can for as little as they can" ("mucho mas por mucho menos"). The irony is that this selfish idolatry may yield early returns, but will result in ultimate losses. Thus, we hear Jesus's paradoxical warning that the first will become last and (good news) the last become first! For if we draw the bottom line at the "almighty dollar," then we haven't gone far enough in drawing the line. "What does it profit someone to gain the world," warned Jesus, "but lose his soul/life?" True Christians and Aggies get the last laugh!

The key to receiving the gift of this wisdom is to embrace prevenient grace. Because grace is God's true love, it is therefore unconditional. It doesn't depend on performance or possession. Real love begins with being, not having or doing. It doesn't say, "I'll love you if . . .," or "I'll love you when . . .," or "I'll love you as long as . . ." True love is "I love you . . . period"! That is why in Christian marriages we vow mutually to love one another as husband and wife, "for richer or poorer, for better or for worse, in sickness or in health"; not just when times are good, but forever, as long as there is mutual commitment. Prevenient means literally "to come before." To be a true Twelfth Man and enjoy the blessings of victorious living, it is important that we show our loving support before our teams do well and not just after. Our sinful human nature is to wait on honoring someone with our love until after they have proven their success. The scriptures say that God loved us before we were saved, "while we were yet sinners" (Romans 5:8). One of the most powerful images offered by Jesus in scripture is His story of the prodigal son who is welcomed back home by a forgiving father who does not shame him for his mistaken choices. Actually just the opposite! The father's love watches for his son's return, then runs to him "while he was still far off." "Filled with compassion," the father "put his arms around him (his son) and kissed him," honored him with a ring and a robe and a party celebrating his return! (See Luke 15, the "Lost and Found Chapter.")

We love effectively only when we do not resentfully wait for preferred behavior, whether it is our spouse, children, employees, team, or whoever. Jesus explained to a conservative, judgmental, legalist that Jesus had shown mercy on a "sinful," errant "woman of the streets" who washed His feet, that, "those who are forgiven the most are those who love the most" (see Luke 7:36–50). When the Twelfth Man resumes chanting "Wrecking Crew" whenever our defense makes an outstanding contribution, the defense will resume playing like the wrecking crew of old. (Since I first started writing this chapter, this prophecy has partially come true!) When we start chanting "Awesome Magic" whenever our offense makes an outstanding play, we will not only be praising the Spirit, but encouraging confidence and momentum, and an even more outstanding offensive performance. We don't wait until after our plants have flowered or borne fruit to water them; we water before, preveniently, and then they bloom and bear fruit. Love people before they do well and especially after they have made mistakes and fallen short, and you will see amazing results! Amazing grace results in amazing glory! This power of prevenient grace again applies as well to parents, bosses, organizational officers, politicians, and leaders in general toward those they lead.

Prevenient grace also includes prevenient faith. That means we not only are to love people before they are successful but also believe in people before they do well. When Coach Krzyzewski of Duke came as a guest in Aggieland and spoke in the Rudder Tower Auditorium on leadership for the building of champions, he emphasized the importance of believing in his players and sharing their vision or dreams. Coach "K" said, "Mutual commitment helps overcome the fear of failure . . . especially when people are part of a team sharing and achieving goals. It also sets the stage for open dialogue and honest conversation." The winning attitude is not so much "I'll believe it when I see it," as "I'll see it when I believe it!" (And say it and feel it!)

When Donna and I had the Aggie Women's Basketball Team at our home in August of 2007, I showed them a couple of video clips from the movie Glory Road, the story of the first "all African-American starters" National Champions basketball team from West Texas State in 1966 whose coach believed in their ability to reach their potential. We then watched a concert performance clip from ABBA as they sang "I Have A Dream," a take-off from the great Reverend Martin Luther King's civil rights speech in 1963. I asked each of the players if they would share their dream. As they did, we all affirmed each other's hopes, and it was a very encouraging experience. I gave each of the young ladies a pocket/purse rock (a polished precious stone) as a reminder of Jesus's promise at the close of His Sermon on the Mount, "Those who hear my words and act upon them will be like the wise man who built his house upon rock," which allowed him and his family to prevail over the various storms we all face (Matthew 7:24). (The second letter of the Jewish alphabet is beth, which means rock and also house/family. When the basketball teams break their huddle, they say the word family.) The rock affirmed, reminded, and helped give depth and breadth to the meaning of their huddle break tradition. The team went on that year to win their first Big Twelve Championship and make it for the first time to the Elite Eight of the NCAA Tournament where they lost to the eventual National Champions Tennessee.

As a pastor, I was privileged to continue studying and teaching (where I learned even more) about many things that help people live better. Especially, I learned more about the importance of the quality of family life. This family systems information was both relevant to our natural family and our families of choice (e.g., our significant groups of friends, teammates, coworkers, classes, church groups, hobby groups, etc.). In particular, I studied the family leadership called "parenting" and "marriage enrichment." I learned a lot from the program "Active Parenting," which emphasizes the importance of encouragement, as well as avoiding discouragement. The word encourage comes from the original meaning "to put heart in" or "give heart." Encouragement is, I believe, the most powerful gift we can give to one another and an expression of our call to "love one another" and to "honor one another." To communicate our love and honor, our appreciation and hope for others is the key to encouraging them. To let them know sincerely and unselfishly that we deeply care about them, that we commend them for their character and achievements, and that we believe in their hopes and dreams, is to give them heart! And amazing things are possible by the power of God's loving Spirit who "is able to accomplish abundantly far more than all we can ask or imagine" (Ephesians 3:20b).

Six years ago, I felt our women's basketball team needed a little extra encouragement going through a tough stretch in conference and a few losses (for Aggies: "getting outscored, running out of time"). Valentine's Day was the next week and a luncheon had been scheduled. I prayed and decided that a Valentine's card was in order. To enhance the encouragement, I personalized it further by adding, "We admire you. We appreciate you. We adore you. Love, Brother Barry." Faith, hope, and love and the encouragement they bring are hard to quantify, and the primary glory always goes to God, but the team certainly has been playing more inspired, winning basketball since then (2010)! And since then they're even calling me "Brother Barry" whenever I see them. The next year (2011), I added a prayer of encouragement to the Valentine's card, and they won a National Championship! (see Appendix).

Usually when we are offering encouragement as a Christian or a Twelfth Man, certain techniques are most helpful, like using the person's first name with a very positive, respectful tone that honors and affirms. I try to give the name "celebrity status." This lets the person know that they are special, (for we are all special in God's eyes). Sometimes a positive (not demeaning) nickname can be an appreciated sign of endearment. For instance, I would yell for Aggie basketball player Joseph Jones with the name "Jo Jo" during his four years here. In 2010, when I wanted to affirm how well freshman Kelsey Assarian was playing as a post who could overcome tough defensive opponents and score, I told her I was giving her the new nickname of "Kickin'": Kelsey "Kickin'" Assarian! She laughed, but seemed to like it, and played even tougher since! I very much enjoyed sitting at the table with her and her family at the banquet when at the end of the season she was named the most improved player.

I also talked with our two leading point guards, Sydney Colson and Sydney Carter, and said, "Einstein had said that e=mc2, but now at A&M, energy equals Sydney C squared!" They since were not only working well in rotation, spelling each other off, but playing great together in tandem! Before the recent Big Twelve Tournament of 2010, I told Danielle Adams, who is even stouter than Kelsey in the post, that I had a new yell for her. I said it was from the new movie Clash of the Titans, where Neptune (Liam Neeson) sends his ultimate weapon, a giant sea monster, against his opponents as he declares, "Release the Kraken!" Danielle smiled and said she liked it. Then that weekend, she played even greater and was named the most outstanding player of the tournament! After beating previously-undefeated Nebraska, Danielle told the media interviewer that she didn't believe that anyone could stop her! "Release the Kraken!"

When people are encouraged, by definition, they have "heart." I have often said to my sons and other young people that I coached and taught that although it is helpful to have physical and athletic talents, the two most important muscles for a champion to possess are the ones inside your ribcage and between your ears: heart and smart. And heart motivates smart! (Although we can also be "smart" in recharging our "heart.")

Now heart can be thought of as having three major characteristics or components: courage, confidence, and commitment. Danielle's statement captures and expresses all three. Courage is "prowess bold" in the face of a difficult opponent: bravery, valor, mettle, and true grit. It is respect without fear. The word courage comes from the Latin word cor, which means "heart." And courage is the most central characteristic of heart.

The second component of heart is confidence. It is similar to courage, but like its root words, "con" (with) and "fides" (faith), implies the strong presence of believing. A person with confidence trusts that there is a spirit (God) that he can count on to guide and energize him or her toward success or victory. He/she has a "can do" attitude that is based on belief in God's blessings. He or she believes that nothing can stop him/her, that with God, all things are possible! (Again see Appendix: "Prayer of Encouragement.")

Finally, the nature of heart must include commitment. There is a devotion that comes from the loyalty dimension of friendship (Ruth). To be committed is to be dedicated to a "won't quit" attitude, a will to persevere. Commitment, for the Christian, is based upon the mutuality of covenant. God makes promises to be there for us as provider and protector, and we are invited to enter that covenant by our promises to love God and others. This covenant relationship is initiated and confirmed in baptism and renewed in holy communion. For the Aggie, this unifying mutuality is celebrated and strengthened in the many of our traditions as Twelfth Men, such as singing "The Spirit" or the "Aggie War Hymn" with its accompanying "Sawing Off of Varsity's Horns" or staying/standing after getting outscored and singing "The Twelfth Man".

Working together unselfishly on many projects of sacrificial service such as Bonfire or "The Big Event" helps develop this sense of commitment. These traditions are an important part of A&M's "other" education. With many Aggies serving in the military, their sacrificial giving has been an example by often taking on heroic "life or death" dimensions of commitment. Just sharing the discipline of knowing, respecting, and observing the many Aggie traditions builds a sense of commitment that enables Aggies to persevere in the face of challenges, even in those adversities that are severe. That is a key reason why so many Aggies have left a great legacy of leadership and generosity!

When my mother suffered a sudden cerebral hemorrhage in 1980 at the young age of fifty-one, the doctors were telling us that there was no brain activity and that we needed to decide to remove life support. I remember looking at her Aggie ring still on her hand and finding "heart" as I thought of the words of the song "The Twelfth Man": "When we're down, the going's rough and tough, we just grin and yell, 'We've got the stuff!'" Of course, I also found comfort and strength through many other means of grace, such as comfort from loved ones, scripture, hymns, and prayers. But my first thought was of that Aggie tradition of the Twelfth Man. And it helped me to carry on bravely in the midst of grief for my Aggie Mom, my first and best early Twelfth Man!

There are some Aggies nowadays, and even back when I was in school, that say they don't like the Twelfth Man song, because they say it is only sung when we lose. I believe they are missing the point! Many students tell me that they don't even know the words! I would say first to them that when we don't quit, we don't really lose, but only get outscored or run out of time. This kind of faith attitude helps us when we face the grief situations in our lives of seeming to lose in various ways: a loved one, our job, our health, our home, a dream, a treasured possession, etc. Especially as a Twelfth Man, we are needed and called upon to "maintain heart" as, again and again, we are there to yell for and not at our teams, to be encouragers and not discouragers. When we lose a fumble or possession of the ball on downs or an interception, do we just grin and yell, "We've got the stuff"? Or do we just groan, shake our heads, roll our eyes, and yell, "You suck!" "Change quarterbacks!" or "Fire the Coach!"? The former is a Twelfth Man, and the latter may be wearing a 12 on his shirt, but is acting like "one- two-percenter."

Jesus warned us of being hypocrites, which literally means "under a mask," and cautioned His followers about wolves in sheep's clothing. My dad taught me at an early age that Aggies don't "boo" their teams, nor do they leave before the game is over when the Ags have fallen behind in the score. Fair-weather fans should have gone to Austin or somewhere else. Jason, our oldest son, while in undergraduate school at A&M, during one of our supportive phone calls to him, commented about the phony nature of some folks. He referred to a line from one of Bob Dylan's songs that we had sung at church camp: "You've got a lot of nerve to say you are my friend. You just want to be on the side that's winning!" Jesus said, "Those who are ashamed of me and of my words, of them the Son of Man will be ashamed when he comes in his glory" (Luke 9:26a). And, "Just as you did it to one of the least of these who are members of my family, you did it to me" (Matthew 25:40b). True Aggies and true Christians are not just fair-weather fans!

After being surrounded by a particularly critical and pessimistic group in the zone as I watched with my younger son Matt a challenging football game against Miami, the half-time highlights video boasted that A&M had the greatest fans in the world. I commented to Matt that perhaps Miami's fans were even better because it seemed that many had disguised themselves in maroon and were up here bad-mouthing our team! When our team was behind in the second half, several got up and started leaving. I commented that they shouldn't be wearing 12 on their jerseys and acting like that (maybe I thought a number 13 more appropriate—a number traditionally assigned to the prince of lies and deception)! We are the best fans when we follow our traditions of loyalty, traditions of a greater love. When we start pointing a finger of blame, we should remember that there are three fingers pointing back at ourselves. As Coach K once said of champions, they "play as a team—they win as a team or lose as a team. Five fingers make a fist!" Do you like to say, "We won!" but when outscored say, "They lost!"?

Some specific Twelfth Man traditions that symbolically illustrate this value are as follows:

- We stand together throughout the game.
- We yell "Fifteen for Team"—fifteen "Rahs" when the Ags score.
- We also whoop it up and kiss our date and high-five our neighbor Ags.
- We also yell "T-E-A-M" when we are scored upon (as a team) (not "You suck!").
- We never "Boo" our team (by the way, yelling "You suck" is the equivalent of booing).
- We stay until the end of the game and sing the "Aggie War Hymn" and "Sawing Off Horns."
- If WE get outscored, we sing "The Twelfth Man" song (learn the words!) and then practice our yells before leaving so to do a better job next time of support (pointing the finger of responsibility at ourselves).
- We maintain our honor and dignity, remembering that "We've Never Been Licked," and we are still Aggies!

After graduating and being commissioned from A&M, I worked first as a mechanical engineer. I then served as an army officer before entering seminary at Perkins School of Theology and ministry through the Southwest Conference of the United Methodist Church. As a young seminarian, I was challenged by my Phenomenology of Religion professor to write my term project on the religion of Texas A&M. I could easily tell that this prof was not going to be respectful of what that paper might say. Like many back then he just thought we were a strange cult! (Not a distinctive ethnicity of diligence, excellence, leadership, loyalty, integrity, hospitality, unselfish service, and respect/honor.) Small group ministry and the human potential/self-actualization/personal growth movement was of great interest to me and less subject to my teachers disdain, so I chose to study that more and report on its religious implications and assumptions.

Another course I was taking at the time about small group ministries revealed the findings of some helpful and exciting research conclusions about the key small group characteristics (and therefore behaviors of participants), which effectively promoted personal growth. Because there were just three, and this seemed a profound insight, I committed them to memory and hopefully learned them by heart. They are non-possessive warmth, accurate empathy, and personal authenticity. Non-possessive warmth is showing affection without strings attached. It is giving without placing requirements on the recipient. Non-possessive warmth excludes an attitude of entitlement! It is loving without all the controlling. Accurate empathy has to do with understanding how the other is feeling and letting them know you perceive their emotions. Personal authenticity means honesty in showing what you think and feel; having integrity in what you say and do and not being phony or hypocritical. It means your walk matches your talk. It is being genuine and sincere.

These characteristics seemed true to my theology and personal experience and have proven themselves effective throughout my years of ministry. They are great goals that accomplish greater goals! They make great love even greater love! Indeed, they seem in many ways to helpfully define what it means to be a Christian friend/family and, similarly, an effective Twelfth Man. If you wish to seek and support excellence in your own life and in the lives of others, to call forth greatness, and if you desire quality of relationship with the people who are most important to you, then I highly recommend remembering, understanding, and pursuing these ways of relating. I believe this is close to Jesus's own example and command/promise to "strive first for the kingdom of God and His righteousness, and all these things will be given to you as well" (Matthew 6:33).

Notes

Chapter 4

Questions for Reflection, Discussion, and Sharing

1. Student athlete E. King Gill became the symbolic first "Twelfth Man" as he unselfishly "stood by" to support and serve as needed. Whose loyalty has supported and inspired you? In your family? In your community? For your country? Fictional character? At Texas A&M?

2. Describe a profile for a great Twelfth Man?

3. Describe a profile of a two-percenter?

4. How was Ruth a biblical prototype of the first Twelfth Man(/Woman)? Why is the term ruthless appropriate for those without loyalty?

5. How does Jesus epitomize the Twelfth Man ideal? On Holy Thursday, after the Last Supper/Passover Meal, Jesus asked His disciples to be the Twelfth Man for him: How did they do when he counted on them? Who are some of those counting on you? Do you count on Jesus? The Spirit? For what? Where would you like to count/lean on Him more?

6. How does Jesus's new name for us, "Friend," free us for victorious living and commission us to be "Twelfth Men"? (Read John 15:12–17.) (Hint: the biblical word for "servants" is literally translated "slaves"!)

7. How does owning the Twelfth Man calling make Aggies a family?

8. How does the literal name of the Holy Spirit, "Paraclete" coincide with the Twelfth Man tradition?
9. How is God, "Father, Son, and Holy Spirit," our best Twelfth Man (e.g., read Psalm 136, "for His steadfast love endures forever")?

10. How does chapter 15 of Luke ("Lost and Found Chapter") emphasize the Twelfth Man approach of loyal love, which supports with honor their own, especially when they are needful? ("When we're down, the going's rough and tough.") Specifically, in the story of the prodigal son, how does the Gracious Father seek to heal the son's shame with sign acts of honor (Luke 15:20–24)? What are some similar Aggie acts of honor?

Our "Home Harvest" in Christ is not only life in our years, but years in our lives. Several family members celebrate with our step-grandmother Winnie her 102 birthday. Although a graduate of UT she embraced the honor aspect of being a Twelfth Man to our family.

Old TAMU Flower Garden

Now the Williams Former Student Center at South Gate, where I proposed to Donna. She said "Yes" and we married at St. Anthony's Catholic Church in August after my senior year (before my last "extra" semester). God helped us continue to flourish, then bear fruit!

My first (and only :-)) wife and love, Donna (shades of Sophia Loren and Annette Funicello!)
(The "beehive" hairdo was popular in the late sixties! - Thankfully some traditions change!)

Matt and Heather's first child, Deacon, at about 2.

Our youngest grandson, Knox at age 6 at Kyle Field.

Matt and Heather.

My younger son, Matt '99, proposing under the Century Tree to his wife Heather in 2004, with his own Ross Volunteers honor guard. They also stood at the recessional of their wedding with a saber arch!

Our oldest son Jason and his wife Janua raising their kids Seth and Olivia Rose right! Most importantly clothe yourselves with Greater Love!

My only "girl", grand-daughter, Olivia Rose at one year.

Jason '94 and Janua '95.

Celebrating our loyal love for A&M and Aggies with Reveille at a softball game.

CHAPTER 5

RUTH, REVEILLE, & BIBLICAL, ZOOLOGICAL PSYCHOLOGY

Before the witness of the apostles in the New Testament, persons of prophetic propensity used stories of animals to convey important truths that might be too confrontational and politically risky were it not for this personification of the creaturely kingdom. An excellent example is that of Aesop and his fables. Hares and tortoises, grasshoppers and ants, lions and mice make excellent points without directly placing blame and shame on the politically powerful and potentially hostile persons who most need to hear and learn from their lessons. So too Jesus, and others of biblical leadership, employed animals to describe character traits and communicate behaviors.

There are many examples from the four gospels where Jesus utilizes images of different animals to express spiritual truths. When our Lord seeks to define His leadership relationship with His followers, He offers one of my favorites, "I am the good shepherd. The good shepherd lays down his life for the sheep" (John 10:11). "He calls his own sheep by name and leads them out" (John 10:3b). "The sheep follow him because they know his voice" (John 10:4b). In Matthew's Gospel, we hear this Good Shepherd Lord caring for those who would follow Him, "See, I am sending you out like sheep into the midst of wolves, so be wise as serpents and innocent as doves" (Matthew 10:16). "Are not two sparrows sold for a penny? Yet not one of them will fall to the ground apart from your Father. So do not be afraid; you are of more value than many sparrows" (Matthew 10:29,31). These are powerful words utilizing the names of various animals to convey very illuminating portraits of personality: a type of biblical, zoological psychology.

Jesus, more than most of us, was something of a student of animal and plant life. In His Sermon on the Mount, he not only uses this knowledge, he also commands us to contemplate its meaning as well when he instructs us to "Look at the birds of the air; they neither sow nor reap nor gather into barns, and yet your heavenly Father feeds them. Are you not of more value than they? And can any of you by worrying add a single hour to your span of life? And why do you worry about clothing? Consider the lilies of the field, how they grow; they neither toil nor spin, yet I tell you, even Solomon in all his glory was not clothed like one of these. But if God so clothes the grass of the field, which is alive today and tomorrow is thrown into the oven, will he not much more clothe you—you of little faith?" (Matthew 6:26–30). The Greek verbs used here are stronger than most realize calling for deeper, philosophical reflection; in other words, not just casual bird-watching or nature-gazing pleasantries. From the first couple of chapters of Genesis, God has been interested in humans noticing and appreciating, naming and having dominion/stewardship over His creatures. And although these creatures are not sufficient for the satisfying companionship of marriage, family, and friendships, they are an important part of our curriculum!

So we may imagine a reptilian regression when Jesus speaks of hypocritical religious leaders by calling them poisonous snakes. As such, they are more in the genus of Satan as the serpent who tempted Eve. Or as wolves in sheep's clothing when they betray their calling and abuse members of Christ's flock. When Jesus himself is baptized, the nature of God's Spirit, which descends upon Him, is likened to that of a dove, not a hawk or a sparrow! If you do bird-watch as Jesus told us to do and pay attention to aviary personalities, you will notice the viciousness of hawks that prey even upon other birds. At times, they kill not just for food, but for the thrill, or just because they can. You will also see that sparrows are not very noble, but greedy, fussy, wasteful, and territorial. They are not very beautiful, loyal, or kind. They are not good team players. Yet our heavenly Father still cares for them. And Jesus said this should give each of us hope! Do you hear/see/understand the message? Though we may have been sparrow-like before accepting Christ as our Savior, through our baptism we can be born again into a spiritual life that looks more like the dove—beautiful and graceful, loving and loyal. As John the Baptist said, let us "bear fruit worthy of repentance!"

On an all-male campus back in 1931, an early year of the Great Depression, some Aggies were returning from a trip to Navasota in an old Model T when they could not avoid hitting and slightly injuring a young, female stray pup. Compassionately, they picked her up and brought her to campus to nurse this mixed breed mutt back to health. Her secret presence was soon compromised when the next morning she loudly greeted the day's bugler with barks and howls as he played reveille. The cadets immediately knew what they would call her, and so the name of the first Aggie mascot, Reveille. My dad used to speak proudly of the way in which Reveille would perform "shepherding duty" on Kyle Field by guarding it, the football team and Aggie Band from opponents' trespassing/desecration, and anyone else not supposed to be on it. She quickly had become a symbol of the loyal, "greater love," which is unselfishly providential and sacrificial in service.

There is no other mascot that better reflects these core values, for the dog has long been known as "man's best friend." She would be an inspiration to the many Aggies who would too soon fight in World War II and future wars. She is honored by freshmen (fish) by the greeting and title, "Howdy, Miss Reveille, Ma'am!" She herself is shepherded by Corps of Cadets outfit E-2, and in particular its sophomore class. Her uniform is a maroon and white Aggie blanket with a five-diamond insignia indicating that she is the highest-ranking cadet in the Corps! She is not a Rottweiler, Doberman, bulldog, or pitbull. Not a poodle, pug, Pekingese, or Chihuahua. And there is a reason. She is more of the form of a Lassie. And though the present day use of a collie has lost some of the meaning of the original Reveille's lack of social stature in high society's eyes (symbolized by t.u.'s "tea sippin'") by being of mixed breed, and probably neglected and abused, (but none the less valued in God's eyes and shepherded by His Spirit), she still represents the fierce and noble loyalty that exemplifies what it means to be a Fightin' Texas Aggie. Reveille's is the same kind of greater love and faithfulness so beautifully portrayed by the biblical character Ruth. Her beauty goes beyond her coat of many colors to the glory of God's loyal love. Her loyalty is her royalty! And as Reveille's name implies, she should still be a "wake up call" to a world that is often ruthless, classist, bigoted, impersonal, selfish, apathetic and uncaring.

We have heard it said that a picture is worth a thousand words. So when we see an outline of a Longhorn steer with its horns severed and hanging down, it speaks volumes about an archrival's character and a purpose and passion for Aggies to BTHO t.u.! To add to the picture scriptural words of promise, "I will cut off the horns of the wicked" (Psalm 75:10) only magnifies the fervent desire to achieve victory over this deserving foe. The Longhorn was an animal that was associated with Texas as a state because of its prominence as a source of food and economic value at one time (the beginning of A&M's history). Longhorn was even the early name of the Aggies' yearbook. Did the Austin folks copy it for their mascot and name, which had been Varsity? Biblically though, the bull calf was a false idol representing mammon, bully intimidation, worldly affluence, sexual priority and pleasure, etc. And, in general, whenever we hear an animal named in scripture, it paints a powerful picture that offers a great deal of insight and emotion into what is being communicated.

Another powerful animal symbol for me personally has been the cardinal. When going through a particularly difficult time in my life a few years ago, I prayed to God for a sign of His presence. I remember looking up and seeing a cardinal. And it happened not once, but many times as I was tempted to despair, discouragement, and depression. God's everlasting love and the power and encouragement that comes with His grace has been revealed in so many ways, but always I feel His special care whenever I see these feathered friends. Cardinals are of course beautiful, but they are more importantly a more noble creature say than sparrows, more peaceful than aggressive, and that exhibits inspiring loyalty to spouse and offspring, unselfishly sharing food, and keeping constant lookout for danger to loved ones. Cardinals continue to inspire and encourage me!

My paternal grandmother was quite a loyal and loving person. She was especially gifted as a singer, who while living as a young adult in Houston used to be a featured singer on Sunday morning at her church and over the radio. Her favorite song which she performed in church choir until late in her life was written by Civilla Martin, wife of evangelist Dr. Walter Martin in 1905. It was a year after she had written her other well-known hymn, "God Will Take Care of You." She and her husband were visiting with another couple, Mr. and Mrs. Doolittle, who had become dear friends. They were also a profound inspiration, for in spite of serious afflictions (she was bedridden, and he worked out of a wheelchair), they maintained a joyful Christian life, bringing comfort and encouragement to others. When asked by Dr. Martin their secret, Mrs. Doolittle's reply was simple: "His eye is on the sparrow, and I know he watches me." Civilla's hymn "His Eye Is on the Sparrow" was the result of that experience, and an expressive second classic hymn that continues to be a much-appreciated source of encouragement for many Christians. After using it to cheer my beloved ill stepmother Loyce, she later chose it for her funeral service and asked that I do the graveside service.

Though Christ has come to the world, not to condemn it but to save it, the Bible speaks of a final judgment that he will bring (see Mathew 25:31–46). There will be eternal consequences for the way in which we have lived our lives. It will mean blessing and bliss for some, and sadness and stress for others. What will make the difference? The Shepherd King, Jesus, said, He will separate people as a shepherd separates sheep from goats. On one hand, the sheep are those who cared for even the least of these who are members of Christ's family as they had need. On the other hand, the goats are those whose sins of omission or commission led them to neglect or abuse the same needful/disadvantaged. For Jesus explains that as we have done or not done it to these, we have done or not done it to Him! Excuses of prejudice, or fiscal conservatism, or whatever, will not get us off the hook! The issue will be whether or not we followed as faithful sheep the voice and way of the Good Shepherd in sharing His sacrificial service and unselfish care for others.

Which are the creatures that inspire and inform us? Do we faithfully follow the Shepherd's voice? Are we loyal like a lamb? Do we receive the Spirit like that of a dove? Do we accept the ideal of Ruth and Reveille of loyal friendship, of God's greater love?

Notes

Chapter 5

Suggested Study/Discussion Questions

1. Name a favorite fable. How does it speak to you?

2. Do you have a favorite animal? Pet from your childhood? Special animal cartoon character? How does it inspire, inform or comfort you?

3. What are some of the ways you enjoy contemplating birds? Flowers? Nature in general?

4. Do you ever find yourself acting "sparrow-like"? Like a dove? Hawkish? In what ways? They say, "Birds of a feather flocks together!" What kind of birds do you like to hang with?

5. What about Reveille appeals to you? How is she a "dog with sweet relish and mustard"?

6. The "Parable of the Final Judgment" (Matthew 25:31–46) suggests that although sheep and goats may appear to be similar, there is an important difference that will have eternal consequences. What is the significant difference?

7. How would you answer the questions at the end of the chapter? Which are animals to avoid imitating?

Walter and Maybeth Bauerschlag '50 at their Ring Dance.

Before our wedding ring ceremony was our Aggie Ring Dance.

Jason and Janua also celebrated before their marriage getting their Aggie rings..

Honoring my fathers and mothers led me many places including my paternal grandmother's childhood home in Mossy Grove; just south of Halletsville.

Next to the Mossy Grove United Methodist Church the cemetery held graves of many pioneers: early settlers of Texas and the oldest graves of Lavaca County.

Near the entrance were the tombstones of my great-grandparents Edward and Margaret Tarkington. His epitaph still inspires, "An honest man is the noblest work of God."

There also a friend and mentor to my great-grandfather, John Livergood, a founding father and hero of early Texas. He and wife Sarah are both buried there at Mossy Grove.

An even older friend of an earlier generation, William Smothers, who fought in the American Revolution and whose son and grandson helped with the Texas War for Independence, was honored nearby with this historical marker.

A portrait of a special Aggie hero, legendary Lieutenant General James Earl Rudder that hangs in Rudder Tower. Commander of the Ranger Battalion on D-Day, June 6, 1944; then he served as President of Texas A&M from 1959-1970 leading her forward from an all-male segregated military college to a co-educational, integrated university with a diverse civilian and ROTC/Corps of Cadets population of over 50,000 students. Principled and progressive, he was a member of A&M United Methodist Church

My grandfather Mr. J. G. "Cub" Barry (educator, coach, administrator, civic, leader) as Superintendent of Hondo ISD. He was on the Baylor basketball team bus of the "Immortal Ten" who died in a train accident going to play t.u. in Austin.

Barry, Bobby, Billy, Maribeth, Melanie, and Holly with my mother, Maybeth at Astroworld (Circa 1966). (My mother was a cousin to the Hofheinz family who built Astroworld and the Astrodome, developed Astroturf and established the Astros team).

A pastor & family photo from our "middle years".

Deacon and Knox at the new Kyle Field.

Seth and Olivia, Deacon and Knox at the Aggie Ring replica with Kyle Field in the background.

Deacon and Knox dressed up for All Saints Eve (Halloween!).

That "70's Look" as I, with Donna, led a youth retreat while attending seminary at SMU.

Election Day in 1972 after Watergate with 4 month old Jason (during first semester of seminary at SMU).

Embracing family life, spiritual education and 70's life after military service during the Vietnam War.

My grandsons Deacon and Knox run the bases at Olsen Field in Bluebell Park after a game with some "Aggie Magic"! The church also celebrates the mysterious and miraculous victories of God.

Knox after winning 3 games at the State Championship.

I was proud of my Dad, Walter H. Bauerschlag, Jr. '50 for many things. Here with my mother her father, Mr. J. G. Barry (hat in hand) where he was chief engineer for the Alaskan Pipeline.

CHAPTER 6

HONOR YOUR FATHER AND MOTHER
& APPRECIATE YOUR AGGIE HERITAGE

An important piece of wisdom enshrined in the Ten Commandments is "Honor your father and mother." This Fifth Commandment is followed with the explanation of consequences and promise of blessing, "so that your days may be long in the land that the Lord your God is giving you" (Exodus 20:12). Honoring others, and especially those in our families who have made a major contribution to our history and heritage, is the key to the fullness and fruitfulness of our own lives. And this should include not just our natural fathers and mothers, but also other significant ancestors and individuals who in the process of our lives have made a memorable difference.

One way of understanding the Bible and many of its books is this concern to honor the relevance of God's loving work through and sometimes in spite of those members of our spiritual/human family who came before us. The scripture tends not to sugarcoat these biographies so that we may not only be inspired by their heroism but also be informed by their humanness. We learn not only from their faithfulness but also from their failures and frailty. Many times as in the stories of the Patriarchs (Abraham, Jacob, Joseph, etc.), it seems even more that we learn from their mistakes. Through Christ, we are given the courage, wisdom, and grace to face and forgive their past sins, even if our family members were neglectful or abusive of us or our loved ones. This honoring with honesty is a healing way we are freed from the influences/consequences we are warned about in the second commandment to descendant generations when our ancestors' faithfulness has faltered (see Exodus 20:4–6). So may we value the importance of knowing, remembering, respecting, and appreciating those who have gone before us, whether in our natural families, our faith families, or in our Aggie family.

We live in an age when the ability to do this commandment is greater than ever before, and yet it is probably more neglected. For although we now have access to biographical information for so many of these, we seldom take time to study and remember, much less honor their lives and contributions. Even when there exists a ritual time to express this honoring such as a holiday, very few would make a passing grade in accomplishing this showing of respect and appreciation. Perhaps Mother's Day, Veterans Day, Christmas, and Easter would be the exceptions. But what about other special "saint days" such as Saint Patrick, Saint Valentine, or Saint Nicolas? Who are the "saints" in your life that should be thanked? What about President's Day, or Martin Luther King Jr. Day, or Earth Day? (Do most young people know who Rachel Carson even is?) Or if you are from Texas, do the dates March 2, March 6, or April 21 have special meaning for you? And if you do know and appreciate something about the "founding fathers" of our nation, state, and church, haven't we neglected the "founding mothers"? Do the photos, paintings, and keepsakes in your home honor your/their heritage? Have you found and observed helpful times to reflect on their many benefits to you? Do you practice rituals of remembrance? In distant and not so distant times, their cemetery locations were close by, even next to the church where families gathered so as to promote the observance of this Fifth Commandment. Does All Saints Day have meaning for you? When was the last time you visited a grave or a memorial site such as the Bonfire Memorial or memorials for Aggies who died or served in wars? Does your home include photos, books, keepsakes, symbols and other ways to help honor their history and heritage? Are stories shared of your ancestors or members of your family tree?

My personal journey influenced my historical appreciation probably more than most. Perhaps destiny had a larger role than simply the decisions that I made. I discovered for example in 1983, while visiting Jerusalem and the Holy Lands, that the day the nation of Israel was reborn on May 14, 1948, was the day of my birth! I was born at the Nix Hospital in San Antonio in the shadow of the Alamo. When I was in first grade in the Alamo Heights ISD, we bought an encyclopedia and a set of the Book of Knowledge. I remember that the first thing I looked up was Davy Crockett! Television and Hollywood helped me appreciate him, William B Travis, and Jim Bowie, as well as other founding father heroes. The school library afforded me the opportunity to learn from their biographies and other outstanding persons. For example, I remember reading about Isaac Newton, Benito Juarez, Jim Thorpe, Black Hawk, Wyatt Earp, and many others. In addition, our pastor used biographical and historical sketches in his preaching, which inspired and informed my ideals.

I only recently took time to research the several wonderful accomplishments of the Texas Governor Preston Smith with whose inauguration I had the privilege to help and serve as a Ross Volunteer. His leadership for our state and the Democratic Party accomplished many noteworthy improvements and reforms. Higher education, criminal justice, highway safety, minimum wage, and drug abuse treatment and prevention were some of the areas his administration addressed. However, I was also reminded of his embroilment in the Sharpstown Scandal stock fraud scheme of 1971–1972. In this computer age of the information super highway, it is much easier to obtain this helpful information, although one must be cautious about accuracy. (I also learned he was a Texas Tech graduate.) Beware that historical accounts are often revised by those presently in power!

One of the rituals we observed in the Corps of Cadets was the learning and quizzing of campusology, which included knowledge of past and present leaders. This included, but was not limited to, sports figures. And, unlike today's sports talk shows, this was primarily used to honor, not criticize, the accomplishments of various Aggie athletes and their coaches. I remember, in contrast, as a young adult stopping at a dorm in Austin and discovering how little they knew or cared who their team was playing that weekend or what they had achieved.

There have been so many uplifting stories of Aggies who have served their school and country that it could fill many books, much less one chapter of this book. They have excelled obviously on the field of play and on the battlefield. But they also have given world-changing leadership from the classroom to the boardroom, from the laboratories of research to the laboratories of community service. From A to Z, Aggies have served nobly in almost every field that you can imagine, from the Army/Air Force and the arts to zoology and zygotes.

What an inspiration it has been for me to research the history of Aggieland! Although I felt that I was fairly familiar with these roots, I discovered day after day new accounts of heroism and unselfish service. Of course, each person has their own story, and each Aggie ring was only won with serious study and sacrifice. And where would most of us be without Aggie Moms (and Dads, and Grandmothers and Granddads)! There are so many that deserve special recognition above and beyond the ordinary. It would obviously not be in the scope of this chapter or book to try and name all or even most or many of these and their accomplishments. But I would urge Aggies to read some of this literature and watch the new video, Aggies: The True Story of Texas A&M. Perhaps in learning about these it may help us better grasp the nature and value of "paying our respects" in this way.

I would share that growing in appreciation of my heritage, whether as a Christian, as a member of my family, as an American, as an Aggie, or even as a member of the human race, has been a continuing, lifelong journey. As a United Methodist minister, I had the privilege and responsibility of serving fourteen different appointments (locations), and at least seventeen different local churches. I grew to know and appreciate better significant contributors to our heritage. For example, in Menard, I served with family to Earl Rudder. In Garwood, I served with the (Danklefs) family of one of the Aggie Muster participants at Corregidor whose face was included there with General George F. Moore in the famous 1946 photo from the

Philippines. In Palacios, the Kubecka family (parents of the year with many Aggie children including a football starter, Billy Kubecka) was active, faithful, and generous.

Learning history and honoring heritage is like one of our favorite family activities: putting together a jigsaw puzzle. Together we turn over the pieces and begin to organize the many parts. Those of a similar pattern or color are grouped together in their respective places. Finding borders and respecting limits is helpful. Also valuable is trying to see the big picture and where and how each piece fits in and connects to others. The more we fit together, the more we appreciate and understand the larger picture, and the easier it is (and more fun) to place and connect new pieces. So learning history and honoring heritage is like getting to see a treasure map from the past. Knowing our past becomes a roadmap guide to future fortunes and finds, complete with warnings of the dangers and obstacles along the way!

The tradition of leadership for the Aggie or Christian is only fulfilled as we have an understanding and appreciation of history. It has been wisely warned that those who fail to know the past are doomed to repeat it!

My personal life and that of my family has been enriched by my awareness of the examples of my natural forefathers and foremothers. These ancestors who were significant branches (or roots) of the family tree made major contributions, not just to our family, but often to our nation and world. How valuable it is if some family member will fulfill the role of gathering and learning and teaching the descendants! I know how much I appreciate my mother and father and my grandparents, aunts, and uncles who made a point to share this family history. I only wish I had heard/learned more when I was young. For though I admired what I knew, I believe I would have had loftier dreams, greater confidence, and stronger motivation if I knew anywhere near what I have learned since then. The accomplishments achieved and tribulations overcome from each branch of the family tree are truly amazing! I find strength, courage, and self-confidence from their heroism and honor. In their gifts, I begin to discover some of my own. I also reach toward humility and learn lessons from their struggles and scars. But although it is crucial to acknowledge and learn from their temptations and mistakes, to honor them calls us to a higher acceptance that goes beyond forgiveness of shameful errors to truly appreciating that which was noble. As St. Paul advised the Philippians, "whatever is true . . . honorable . . . just . . . pure . . . lovely . . . commendable . . . excellent . . . worthy of praise, take account of these things" (Phil. 4:8 portions). This is a commendation of Spiritual Accounting 101!

My own dad's honors began at a young age with hard work, ambition, intelligence, good humor, humility, and respect for others and for what was right. Walter H. Bauerschlag Jr. also had a lot of encouragement from home and from my Aggie Mom. For although he was a three-year all-district football player and class president at San Marcos High School, it was his father and mother and my cheerleading mom who was elected Football Sweetheart who gave him such loving support! A class of '50 TAMC civil engineering graduate, he laid pipeline all over the country with Aggie boss H. B. Zachry '22. My dad then built roads, bridges, and freeways with the Texas Highway Department and Aggie bosses Ray Stotzer '46 and Ray Lindholm '45. He finally worked with Brown and Root and Aggie boss Delbert Ward '32, becoming vice president over South American projects and chief engineer of the Alaska Pipeline along the way. But his greater honor was becoming a more loving family man and sending six kids through college (all Aggies of course, except for my oldest sister who went to U of H, then married one of my outfit buds, Max Melcher '70). Even more credit should go to my Aggie mom, Maybeth Barry Bauerschlag, who was the real embodiment of Twelfth Man Spirit. Their faith in Christ and loyalty in His Church meant even more when they both passed on "too young," both in their fifties.

Without any projecting of arrogance, I think it is important to honor our family members with a praise that appreciates their value, then and now. Embrace thankfulness and humility for our heritage, even if we honestly have to work hard sometimes to overcome their mistakes. Jeremiah 31:29–30 is forthright about this challenge. We are not to simply blame our parents and ancestors for our woes, but may acknowledge the poor patterns we are freed in Christ to overcome. They are not just our destiny to accept, but to rise above. And one step in victory is often to acknowledge them and take responsibility for our own decisions, seeking grace along the journey.

So I give thanks for my paternal grandparents who gave wise and unselfish leadership to their family and community in the San Marcos area. I am likewise grateful for his father and grandfather who did the same around New Braunfels after immigrating from the area of Hannover, northern Germany in the late 1860s. My great-great-grandfather Frederick Bauerschlag built houses along the Guadalupe River, while my great-grandfather Heinrich (Henry) farmed near the area of Redwood where my grandfather, Walter Henry Bauerschlag Sr., developed and owned the businesses: a general store, a dairy farm, a blacksmith shop, an auto repair, and a cotton gin. His wife, my grandmother Marguerite (I called her "Chi Chi" from a children's song she sang to me about a chicken) was a strong and loyal family member who had taught school in her younger years in Houston and was an outstanding singer in her church choir, singing on the radio for their services. Chi Chi's dad, Edward Tarkington, had farmed and ranched south of Halletsville at Mossy Grove, where he was a founding trustee of the Methodist Church with other pioneers, founding fathers, and mothers. He was a state legislator for two terms at the turn of the century (she remembered him as a girl riding off on his horse to Austin), after having served as an officer in the Confederate Army and before that as a Texas Ranger. Chi Chi's mother's first husband died young as so many did serving as a Methodist circuit rider from the Missouri frontier area.

On my mother's side, I have discovered even more inspirational heirloom treasures! Both of my maternal grandparents were wonderful people from outstanding families whose faithfulness brought blessing to their descendants as God promised His People in the Ten Commandments. Her folks grew up in Smithville, Texas, where her grandfather, former Englishman Marcus Tansey, was the chief teller of the successful Hill Bank and a leader in the Methodist Church. My grandfather, James Gordon Barry, was the youngest of three boys and a girl born to an outstanding teacher/coach/school superintendent for whom the football field was named (Barry Field in Tiger Stadium, seen in the Sandra Bullock/Harry Connick Jr. movie Hope Floats). My maternal grandfather, known as "Cub" Barry went to Baylor University where he also became an educator/coach/administrator. In 1927, he was on the varsity basketball team when they were traveling by bus to Austin to play the Longhorns on a rainy winter day. In Round Rock, they were hit by a train at the crossing near the station. Although my grandfather survived with minor wounds, four were killed instantly and six more soon died. They became known as The Immortal Ten and are a continuing inspiration today through Baylor traditions including a memorial with statues dedicated in 2007 on campus.

After graduating later that year, Gordon "Cub" Barry was hired as a teacher and the head coach in Bastrop, where they named the teams the Barry Bears after him. They are still the Bastrop Bears. He laughed jokingly about how when they played and defeated his dad's Smithville team that year that his dad would not speak to him for a week! He was hired the next year to be principal and head coach in Hondo, Texas. He was so effective and popular that the following year he was promoted to school superintendent. By 1930, he had composed a fight song for Hondo, which began, "For

Hondo's honor and glory we will fight on, we will be fighting when the day is done and when the dawn is breaking we will still be fighting . . ." And like the Aggies, in 1939, he too won a major championship! His Fighting Hondo Owls baseball team defeated teams from even large schools in Austin and Dallas to win the State Championship, and he was named the state Coach of the Year. He helped Hondo into the football play-offs more than any other school in the state. They also had a very high graduation rate, even from college. And he helped send many athletes to the Southwest Conference colleges/universities and even professional ranks! He was also a leader in Texas public schools in integration of students and faculty, becoming nationally recognized in 1955 to fully integrate Hondo's public schools. I was a very proud grandson and first grader then, but even prouder now!

But a more recent inspiration has been the discoveries about my great-grandfather Barry's great-grandparents, Andrew and Kate Moore Barry. My mother had mentioned that they were involved in the Revolutionary War and that their son and grandson had migrated from South Carolina west across the South (Alabama and then Mississippi) and were both doctors. But it was only a few years ago as I attended a United Methodist National Congress on Evangelism in Myrtle Beach that I took a couple of extra days off to research this part of my family's past.

I had found in 1992, with my wife, Donna and son, Matt, on a patriotic/ heritage "car vacation" to Washington, DC that the old family home in Roebuck, just south of Spartanburg, had been turned in 1961 into a national historical site, and now I was eager to learn more of my ancestors. I soon came to realize that their historical impact was major and much greater than I had known. Kate's father, Charles Moore, had been given a land grant to their plantation (Walnut Grove). As a well-educated man from Great Britain (he had gone to one of the seven ancient universities there), he started the first school in that area, the Rocky Springs Academy, which stayed open from 1770 to 1850. He had ten children beginning with

Margaret Catherine "Kate" Moore in 1752. She was married in 1767 at age fifteen to twenty-one-year-old Andrew Barry who was serving as a local judge. They were patriots, who with their families, supported the American Revolution. She served as a spy against the British and their loyalist supporters, the Tories; he as a commander of the militia or volunteer Patriot forces. At the Battle of Cowpens, which was the turning point of the Revolution, with a decisive defeat of the British forces, Kate is said to have spied and discovered the impending attack from the "Bloody" Lt. Col. Banastre Tarleton. She, being an expert horsewoman, rode twenty-three miles, on her horse Dolly crossing the swollen Pacolet River to warn her husband and the Patriot forces. Andrew Barry was one of four militia company commanders who with Brigadier General Daniel Morgan stayed up that cold January 17 night of 1781 making battle plans and with Kate's help "spiriting up" the troops! Their decisive victory at Cowpens devastated (BTHO) the British troops and indeed "spirited up" the Patriots throughout the colonies and their whole cause for democratic independence. Talk about Twelfth Man support and the power of "greater love" encouragement!

The rest, as they say, is history. A more complete picture is given in the book A Devil of a Whipping, which was loosely used to make the Mel Gibson movie The Patriot! I discovered that the DAR (Daughters of the American Revolution) chapter in Spartanburg named for Kate Barry had just succeeded in getting the main street/road (Highway 29) through the city (similar to Texas Avenue in Bryan-College Station) renamed Kate Barry Boulevard! It is close to the route that she would have traveled to Cowpens in 1781. I also discovered her only portrait on an ivory broach at the local museum. It was donated by another descendant, Amanda Blake, who was better known as "Miss Kitty" on television's historic series, Gunsmoke! In other words, I also found that my family and I were distant cousins with a favorite celebrity!

I hope that this personal account will not only encourage my natural family, but also each reader who loves liberty, country, and state to find ways to explore their own heritage and fulfill the biblical directive to honor your father and mother!

Many spots on A&M's campus give tribute to those who have made major contributions and, by themselves, add to the sense of honor, which is a foundational value/tradition for Aggies. They include buildings named after A&M presidents, deans, professors, distinguished alumni, Medal of Honor winners, Hall of Famers, etc., to many statues and memorials for those whose names are synonymous with wise leadership and courageous, unselfish service. In this age of Internet smart phones and laptops, we have much quicker and easier access to each of their stories. And as the years go by, more and more is being written about our shared heritage. All of this brings esteem and incentive to the larger Aggie family. And a healthy pride propels us to perpetuate excellence!

Many special events such as sports games, Parents' Weekend, the Big Event, and Muster also offer opportunities to express praise and appreciation to Aggies, our fathers and mothers, and others who serve in these ways. Students begin learning quickly that this is one important way of fulfilling our role and duty as a Twelfth Man. It becomes clearer that the power of encouragement is appreciated by our athletes, armed forces members, and alumni/former students ("old Ags") when we practice this form of support. And a ripple effect spreads that encouragement of honor in ever-widening circles throughout our communities and world! For example, when I give leadership to the fans at an Aggie Women's Basketball game and act as a catalyst for crowd enthusiasm, support, and appreciation, I see the ripples of respect and discipline touching the teams and players of many, many schools throughout the Brazos Valley, the state of Texas, Big XII area (now SEC), and beyond! It becomes visible through the quality of competition, but most importantly in the character of the kids and the teachers who coach them! Just as each stone thrown into a pool makes an impact, so each Christian, each Aggie, makes a difference through acts of honoring encouragement! The Bible says it is important to do such for "one another." And our Aggie traditions also tell us to embrace this "power of twelve"! Blessings are promised to follow!

Notes

Chapter 6

Questions for Reflection, Discussion, and Sharing

1. Can you name the Ten Commandments? Where does the commandment to honor our parents come?

2. What are some things that you appreciate about your mother and father? Have you told them?

3. What of your grandparents and earlier ancestors are you thankful and proud of? Have you told them?

4. What about the history of the Aggie family are you most proud and thankful? How can you show it?

5. Who in your biblical family brings you the most inspiration and comfort: Old Testament? New Testament? Why?

6. What are some ways that you honor those in your historical tree? How have you learned of their contributions and heroism? How can you help pass along the tradition of honoring their stories (histories)?

7. How does Aggie Muster serve in this way for the Texas A&M family?

8. Describe how the "jigsaw metaphor" works for you in learning and appreciating history? Other subjects?

9. What do you think of Spiritual Accounting 101, Philippians 4:8?

10. Refer to the "TLC Prayer" song (see appendix) and name an example of each of the nine categories of blessing exalted in this prayer.

Matt's Graduation Day celebrated with family, here Janua and Jason.

Matt was torch corporal as a sophomore making the torches for the Fighting Texas Aggie Band drum majors. He and the Yell Leaders also carried them to Bonfire. His nickname "Torch Boy" is on his torch.

Our youngest son, Matt, as a fish and as a senior in the Fighting Texas Aggie Band. Boys to men!

fish Bauerschlag (Matt) '99 with his Aggie Mom on Parents Weekend! Another of our great Aggie traditions!

Winning pitcher Lauren Ainsley and catcher Megan May after their Regional Championship.

Power hitter/ first baseman/ catcher Nicole Morgan.

2013 Home run and batting average leader, freshman Callie Lanphear.

Outstanding third baseman, "Grand Slam" Amber Garza.

After winning regional in 2013 over Baylor some happy leaders on the Aggie Softball team: Captain Cassie Tysarcyk.

*Excellence in athletics and academics go hand in hand. A team effort includes terrific coaches, tremendous administrators, talented & dedicated athletes, and of course the Twelfth Man overflowing with **optimistic encouragement** and **enthusiastic support**. Many serve on the sidelines and in the background as the Aggie family of success.*

Here with one our best, Aggie Softball Head Coach Jo Evans.

Summertime break after the game with Seth and Olivia a few years ago in Hillsboro. Coaching our kids a great family tradition!

With "heart and smart" and a lot of hard work my oldest grandson Seth and best friend Caden celebrate a fourth state championship with their team, The Waco Storm.

Leading Christmas caroling and singing for those in need (children, ill, elderly, recently widowed, etc.) is a ministry tradition that I was introduced to in Company F-1 and have continued over the years.

CHAPTER 7

LABORERS FOR THE HARVEST
& THE AGGIE WORK ETHIC

Song "The Twelfth Man"

When we're down the going's rough and tough
We just grin and yell, "We've got the stuff!"
To fight together for the Aggie dream
We're the Twelfth man on the fightin' Aggie team!

Aggies have a tradition and reputation for being hard workers. They take seriously their responsibilities for accomplishment and as role models. Aggies hold high the ideals of leadership and excellence with integrity. Their student lifestyle of course has always involved being graded for their class work, studies, and performance on tests and exams. This encourages and even demands a strong work ethic. But life as an Aggie also includes accountability in the "other education" (participation in student and work organizations, especially in leadership responsibilities). In the Corps of Cadets, military training of underclassmen, primarily by upperclassmen who held supervisory responsibilities, stressed performance. But it also emphasized dedication to one's classmates and to A&M, Texas, and the United States. These supervisors reinforced this emphasis with positive and negative consequences. Faithful completion of duties, knowledge of "campusology" and "Aggie facts," attention to details for inspections and drills, and loyal dedication were always priorities. And if someone failed in these areas, there was almost always some upperclassman there to enforce discipline, such as pushups, shoes to shine, additional duties, etc., along with a "not so pleasant" verbal reprimand. You see, in wartime, out at the bonfire site, or eventually in one's vocational responsibilities, failure to do one's duties could easily result in serious harm or casualties. Whether in engineering, agriculture, military, or even sports, fulfilling one's work responsibilities sometimes meant even life or death consequences! So probably, these were some primary roots of the Aggie work ethic.

Recently, my wife Donna and I went to a Western movie (commonly shown when we were young, but not many are still made) Appaloosa, which was set in Appaloosa, New Mexico, in 1888. What occurred to me was the tremendous cultural changes that developed between that time and the present. But what was extra amazing for me to realize was how recently generation-wise these changes had happened and how they had impacted the American work ethic. I had recently turned sixty, being born in 1948. I was a child of the Fifties, a teen of the Sixties, a young adult of the Seventies, mid-life adult of the Eighties, etc. (a.k.a. a baby boomer). I grew up with television and rock 'n' roll, color movies, high-powered cars, suburban conveniences, the Bomb and Cold War, Vietnam, various civil rights and progressive reform movements, the space program and astronauts walking on the moon, etc., and considered myself "modern," working at becoming "postmodern." What I was surprised to realize (doing the simple "Aggie" math) was that those who were sixty (my age) when I was born were themselves born into this world of 1888!

When they wanted to go somewhere, they didn't just make sure they had gas in their car. They either walked or had a horse to care for, train, saddle up, or hitch up (to a wagon or buggy) and know how to ride! They didn't get their milk at Walmart but had to milk a cow that also had to be cared for. Same with eggs for breakfast and tending chickens. Same with preparing fruits and vegetables and growing a garden and tending fruit trees and doing the work of harvesting (and canning) in season. My point is that there used to be a lot of relational responsibility in surviving and thriving that required a strong work ethic. The reality of these relationships also provided support and additional motivation, i.e., there were those we cared about who depended on us and our being responsible and disciplined. I know I felt this to some degree being the oldest of six children with Dad often being away with his job. My mom and younger siblings needed my help. This old-fashioned work ethic was handed down from my grandparents' generation but was not always received in the more modern cultural climate. In this postmodern electronic media age, the temptation is even greater to neglect and ignore relational responsibilities. But because of the respect for tradition and the honoring of elders at A&M, as well as rules, rituals, and reasons aforementioned, much of this emphasis on work ethic has been and is still taught and in place at Aggieland!

From the Christian perspective, there are many admonitions to be diligent in our work. The Lord's prayer asks, "Thy will be done," an emphasis on action to accomplish God's purpose. Jesus's new commandment to "Love one another as I have loved you" also points us to an image of an action verb, Christ caring for people in life-changing ways. Love is not just a noun or even a passive verb. Jesus honored the Father by serving people at their situations of need. We are to do likewise: "Let love be genuine; hate what is evil, hold fast to what is good; love one another with mutual affection; outdo one another in showing honor. Do not lag in zeal, be ardent in spirit, serve the Lord" (Romans 12:9–11). The early church was exhorted to work in the right way and for the right reasons: "Do not be deceived; God is not mocked, for you reap whatever you sow. If you sow to your own flesh, you will reap corruption from the flesh, but if you sow to the Spirit, you will reap eternal life from the Spirit. So let us not grow weary in doing what is right, for we will reap at harvest time, if we do not give up! So then, whenever we have an opportunity, let us work for the good of all, and especially for those of the family of faith" (Galatians 6:7–10). Christians are then "Laborers of the Harvest!"

The Bible warns that the works of Christians actually may be impressive in terms of eloquent witness, insightful prophecy, spiritually wise counsel, miracle-making faith, and acts of tremendous personal sacrifice, yet accomplish nothing unless our works are undergirded by God's grace, filled with His greater love. Saint Paul proclaims, "If I speak in the tongues of mortals and of angels, but do not have love, I am a noisy gong or clanging cymbal. And if I have prophetic powers, and understand all mysteries and all knowledge, and if I have all faith, so as to remove mountains, but do not have love, I am nothing. If I give away all my possessions, and if I hand over my body so that I may boast, but do not have love, I gain nothing" (1 Corinthians 13:1–3). So we are encouraged to embrace true love, His greater love, so that our work does not become an idol, but a means of experiencing and sharing in the true God. Our works become expressions of life-giving righteousness, and we become instruments of His peace (wholeness, abundantly fruitful harvest)! Working in His love by His gracious Spirit, we enjoy the power and glory of His victorious living! Not that we may boast except in His power to accomplish great things (even, and especially through us)! God's wise word to those in leadership is still: "Not by might, nor by power, but by my spirit" (Zechariah 4:6b).

Jesus offers in His Sermon on the Mount a great collection of insights and incentives to do the work of the Father, yet not apart from a faith relationship with Him. So he concludes with this work a warning, "Not everyone who says to me, 'Lord, Lord,' will enter the kingdom of heaven, but only the one who does the will of my Father in heaven. On that day many will say to me 'Lord, Lord, did we not prophesy in your name, and cast out demons in your name, and do many deeds of power in your name?' Then I will declare to them, 'I never knew you; go away from me, you evildoers'" (Matthew 7:21–23). (Did you notice that the works mentioned for credit were more conservative, critical acts of judgment, rather than caring acts of relational helping, and healing/redemption?)

So it is God's powerful love working through us through faith, but not without our active participation. This is the kind of work that God desires of us. Faith is a four H project and four-dimensional. Faith is believing with our heads, having courage in our hearts, sharing kind and caring hands, and living in homes filled with honor and respect. Love is to be understood and trusted, but also lived out and shown to others. James, brother of Jesus, emphasizes, "Be doers of the word, and not merely hearers who deceive themselves" (James 1:22). And again, "What good is it, my brothers and sisters, if you say you have faith but do not have works? If a brother or sister is naked and lacks daily food, and one of you says to them, 'Go in peace, keep warm and eat your fill,' and yet do not supply their bodily needs, what is the good of that? So faith by itself if it has no works, is dead" (James 2:14-17). Yet the warnings of Jesus's words are not without promise. And so the final words of Jesus's Sermon on the Mount both caution about the consequences of inactivity, but also grant the blessings of victorious living for an active and applied faith, "Everyone then who hears these words of mine and acts on them will be like a wise man who built his house on rock. The rain fell, the floods came, and the winds blew and beat on that house, but it did not fall because it had been founded on rock. And everyone who hears these words of mine and does not act on them will be like a foolish man who built his house on sand. The rain fell and the floods came, and the wind blew and beat against that house, and it fell—and great was its fall" (Matthew 7:24–27).

A chapter on the Christian and Aggie work ethic would not be complete without a few words about the Sabbath and the need to observe God's regular rhythm of rest and renewal time. This redemptive downtime is as biblically foundational as the story of creation where God works at creating the universe and the garden planet Earth, then rests on the seventh day, commanding us to do likewise. In the Mosaic list of the Ten Commandments, the call to remember and keep the Sabbath holy is the fourth rule listed, integral to the priority of God Himself (the first three commandments), and prefatory to the respectful treatment of others (the last six commandments). If we are to put God first, it is essential to take this important time out to contemplate the Creator. If we are to honor others, their health and well-being, their appropriate sexual boundaries, their property, their reputations, or even refrain from strongly considering violating these rights, it is equally essential for us to discipline ourselves to the ritual habits of renewal and ensure that others enjoy this same privilege (see Exodus 20:8–11).

In the gospels, Jesus himself gave us a good example of sabbatical rest. Though he worked hard teaching and healing many, he was also a good role model at frequently taking time out for prayer and fellowship, retreat time for worship and close relationships, regularly going on vacations from the crowds and the stresses of doing ministry, often with His disciples. He called those who would be overly rigid and legalistic concerning Sabbath downtime to be more flexible. Even Sabbaths are no time to leave an ox in the ditch or child in a well. He said that the Sabbath was made for people and not the other way around. Jesus declared that he Himself was the Lord of the Sabbath! (see Matthew 12:1–14; Mark 2:23–28; Luke 6:1–11; etc.).

Returning to the Aggies, I remember our oldest son, Jason, who reported to me and his mother as a freshman that Aggies liked to have fun with their friends and knew how to have a good time, but that their studies and other responsibilities came first. He was developing the discipline of taking care of himself, studies, and others in a timely order, honoring balance and boundaries, patience and priorities. He had fun and made good friends, but he also made his grades and gave great service to his school and community, graduating with high honors and as a highly successful officer (Fund Raising Chairperson) of his class! Fighting (working) together for the Aggie dream! We of course were very thankful, humbled, and proud Aggie mom and dad.

Notes

Chapter 7

Questions for Reflection, Discussion, and Sharing

1. Name some of the people who have worked hard for you (family, friends, teachers, coaches, teammates, pastors, neighbors, political leaders, community leaders and volunteers, artists, pets, etc.)? Are there some you have taken for granted? What does the phrase "It takes a village" mean?

2. Who are some Aggies that have worked hard for you?

3. What are some changes in our culture that have affected our work ethic?

4. What does the Bible say to you about work (e.g., Galatians 6:7–10)?

5. What are dangers of thinking hard work alone will save us?

6. Can you name the Four H's of spiritual work projects that bring an abundant harvest of blessings? Give examples?

7. What is the danger of "faith without works"?

8. How is a good work ethic implied in the "Parable of the Houses Built on Rock or Sand"?

9. What do you think it means that Jesus is "Lord of the Sabbath"?

10. What are your cycles/rituals/traditions of work and Sabbath/renewal? How would you like to improve on them?

Growing is a gift from God we can share with our communities as co-creators. Gardening is a hobby and lifestyle which can help us grow in character and wisdom as well.

Everything Grows with Greater Love. A new flowerbed I planted in 2008. The "Agriculture" tradition is both fun and foundational! We nurture flowers and faith!

Home Harvest Ministries emphasizes the abundant life that Jesus promises and produces. The foundational fruits of the spirit are: love, joy, peace, patience, kindness, generosity, faithfulness, gentleness, and self-control. (Gal. 5:22) It is of course practically rewarding when the vegetable garden starts producing also.

The tradition of celebrating Christmas begins with the biblical story of the birth of baby Jesus in Bethlehem. We use an olive wood stable we bought in the Holy Lands, and unbreakable characters that can be safely placed by grandchildren or children at church.

Our family Christmas traditions usually included an Advent wreath (on coffee table). (circa 1988)

Christmas with my siblings my senior year of high school (Alamo Heights). Bobby and I were wearing our Aggie sweat shirts. Front row l to r: Maribeth, Melanie, Billy and Holly.

*Other Christmas/
Christian symbols
around the hearth and
tree have served as
spiritual reminders of
meaning and purpose.*

*Christmas tree decor
is aesthetic but
primarily symbolic,
both of the original
incarnation (God's
Spirit becomes flesh)
but of present day
incarnations. The
bell is a traditional
symbol of incarnation,
and our ATM bell in
a "Maroon & White"
section of our tree is
one of our favorites.*

At the front & center
of our Christmas tree
is the scriptural scroll
announcement of Christ's
"Good News", Lk 2:14.

Yakoff Smirnoff, a
Russian immigrant
comedian at Branson
has honored our
country's greatness.
The autographed
"Stars and Stripes"
tie Donna got
me is one I enjoy
wearing as an
election judge and
on patriotic holidays.
More meaningful
traditions!

This "Veteran's
Memorial Museum"
in Branson Mo.
caught my attention
not just because it
honors those who
served, but because
of the "Red Tail" P29
plane with my wife's
name, "Donna K".

The second letter B of the Hebrew alphabet is pronounced "Beth" and is the word for rock, also meaning house-home-family, an important spiritual symbol, hence our rock garden in front of our home in B-CS or Aggieland.

By the end of the summer our Creator God had helped this Aggie Rock Garden flourish.

Family Traditions: The Chicken Oil Co (carved table) holds a family decorated cake (Aggie Ring crest) for a niece's gradation (Betsy Bauerschlag '11). (Maroon velvet cake inside).

Kids are ready to see their first Bonfire burn!

My two oldest grandchildren., Seth and Olivia, enjoy their first Aggie bonfire in 2012. This "burning desire" to "BTHO" symbol is still a treasured tradition in Aggieland.

While all are created equal and deserve our respect, support and appreciation, football has always held a special place in Aggie history and tradition. These photos depict recent celebrations and dimensions of our traditions. Here is a scene from "First Yell" 2012, the seasons first major yell practice.

Here, at Kyle Field in 2012, the Fightin' Texas Aggie Band honors our entry into the SEC, The Southeastern Conference.

A long standing tradition, the "Block T" is renewed with all the Corps of Cadets and Fightin' Texas Aggie Band and its unity on Kyle Field.

A newer tradition, First Yell helps fund Yell Leaders and their travel to games. Here are Texas Dance Hall Legends: Johnny Bush, Gary P. Nunn and Joe Ely who had followed Aggies Roger Creager '93 and Max Stalling '89 at the 2014 event.

CHAPTER 8

THE ROLE OF RITUALS &
IMPORTANCE OF AGGIE TRADITIONS

R ituals and traditions play an important role in the life of any community. The Bible and Christ specifically point to the ultimate importance of having a right relationship with God and others, and the word that describes this ideal is righteousness. Righteousness is loving the Lord, our God, with all our heart, soul, mind, and strength, and our neighbor as ourselves, a greater love. It is not about being perfect in our appearance, thinking, or behavior or by making everything right. Righteousness is a gift and declaration by God when we believe and trust in Him. Like God declared with Abraham (Genesis 15:6), and Paul reminded us (Romans 3:21–5:11; Galatians), because of our faith we will be reckoned as righteous, and our life approved by God. By this faith, Abraham's life, though obviously imperfect and dotted with mistakes, was not only approved by God, but blessed, and was blessed to bless others! And through faith in Christ we are made heirs of Abraham and this same covenant promise.

Religion is about the organized activity to help persons come to this faith and love and (therefore) fulfillment of righteousness. To do this, religion embraces three major r's: rules, reasons, and rituals. Each one is important and has its role. But they are only important and right as they lead individuals and communities toward righteousness. To try to place ultimate importance on any of the three r's is the mistake of idolatry, that is, trusting something less than God to do what only God can do! In other words, righteousness is the only capital R, while reasons, rules, and rituals are all small r's! The Bible and Jesus condemned idolatry as a futile misplacement of our priorities. Christ warned us not to "major in the minors"! We may be used to thinking of idolatries only as the worship of wealth, pleasure, or fame, that is, materialism, hedonism, and egotism. But the religious have other tempting idolatries. The importance of right reasoning is affirmed in orthodox (original root meaning: "right praise") doctrine. But making this penultimate an ultimate is to commit the mistaken idolatry or sin of doctrinalism. We are not saved solely by our thoughts, as important as they are, but by our faith relationship with God—our righteousness.

The same goes with our rules or laws. Jesus explained, for example, that the Sabbath is made for man and not man for the Sabbath and that he was Lord of the Sabbath. To try to make the Law ultimate is to commit the idolatry/sin of legalism. As important as the law is, it is inadequate by itself to save us (Romans 1-8).

Once more, it is likewise with our traditions. As a matter of fact, the same teaching about the Sabbath applies here, for the Sabbath is both a rule and a tradition or ritual. This idolatry is called ritualism or traditionalism. Time after time, Jesus warned Pharisees and other religious leaders about these mistaken distortions about the proper place and role of religious activities, guidelines, and beliefs.

I have found myself trying to correct some worship leaders, lay, and clergy, who sought to lead a congregation in an affirmation of faith such as the Apostles Creed when they are suggesting that it is what we believe about God, rather than believing in God, that is important. For example, the creed says, "We believe **in** . . .," not just believe **that** . . . ! Trusting God personally, relationally, always trumps trying simply to know and follow things about God, as important as that is! For it is by grace through faith that His Spirit, His truth, and His love is made incarnate in us.

The rules, reasons, and rituals of any community then are vitally important in helping His Spirit to define, create, and sustain its identity, direction, and life together. They inform us about who we are, what we are to do, and why. They inspire us to reach for our purpose and achieve appropriate goals. These should bring glory to God and honor to Him, our families (natural and chosen), and ourselves, for each of us is important and His royal ambassador (John 17). Ultimately, they enhance our righteousness or right relationship with God and others and therefore also our witness.

The special role of traditions and the rituals they describe/proscribe is that they help us to appropriate and apply the important rules and reasons and the core values they embrace. When Jesus, at the end of the Sermon on the Mount, described the righteousness reward of victorious living, He told a story of two choices. Those who would listen to His commandments and teachings (rules and reasons) and apply them (ritual habits/traditions) were compared to someone wise who built his home on a solid, rock foundation. When the inevitable storms of life beat upon that home . . . it prevailed. The wise person's home overcame the challenges to its well-being. It still stood, and it stood still! It survived and thrived! The wise person was/is blessed with victorious living! Not so for the foolish builder who heard Jesus's teachings and commandments but did not act upon them and who then relied on shifting sands (e.g., selfish or self-reliant, worldly, Darwinian-based philosophies of bullying, greed, superstitions, etc.) for a foundation. This is chasing after that which glitters which is not gold. It is "leaning on the never-lasting charms" instead of the "everlasting arms." Or as another song once confessed, "Looking for love in all the wrong places"! Although the storms were for the most part the same for both home builders, the home of the foolish builder fell and failed greatly! Serious stuff!

On our trip to the Holy Lands, Donna and I got to see firsthand the practical illustration Jesus used as He taught on the northern shore of the Sea of Galilee near Capernaum. Violent storms pounced suddenly from the lake's eastern edge's cliffs (the Golan Heights) as cold air from the high altitude would rapidly plummet down to the warm water below and dramatically changed the real estate values as one moved from granite-based land to the unstable, sandy soil of the north-western seashore beach areas. The image Jesus had used was graphic!

The trick for us is to see the truth to which Christ's words point and to follow their proscriptions. That is, to "know Him," the Living Word, "more clearly, to love Him more dearly, and to follow Him more nearly" (traditional prayer from Richard of Chichester, England, thirteenth century, popularized by the musical Godspell. UMH 493). It is important to listen, but even more so to learn to do it. That is to discipline ourselves to "act upon": not just to hear His Truth, but also to embody it. To walk the talk. To appropriate, apply, and practice God's guidance. That is the essence of this book. That encouragement is its purpose.

Why? Because that same wisdom applies to Aggie traditions. They exist for this purpose: to help us live out their core values of a responsible and joyful relationship with the Spirit (of God, of Aggieland), with oneself, and with others. In other words, their purpose is to embrace righteousness. So when we practice a particular tradition, we are most blessed when we grow to understand what it is we are trying to accomplish and teach others.

And when we know how to apply these principles to the many life situations that we face, we will find satisfaction and success in living. We will have embraced and enjoyed victorious living. Our higher education will have helped us know and imitate our higher power.

Assorted and Miscellaneous Traditions

Three basic traditions of Texas A&M are educated excellence in agriculture, engineering, and military science. These embrace the life skills of growing, building, and defending/fighting/overcoming. And each is also a biblical metaphor for a life of Christian discipleship.

Growing

Aggies and Christians are gardeners of good and nurturers of new life in God's greater love. As we read from page one of the Bible, God is the Creator of heaven and earth, and in particular an ideal garden in which he intends for us to live. All of these, He calls "good!" As God creates us humans in His image to be companions/helpmates or family/friends in His garden, He declares us "very good!" A key purpose of God's creation is sharing in the stewardship or management of gardening. We discover our purposeful and meaningful life as we care together for God's creatures and grow His garden, the Earth. God grants us, humans, dominion or authority in the pursuit of this shared task. That is wise stewardship care of the crops, landscape, and livestock, but also providential protection and support for the entire ecosphere! The first commandment of the Bible, to "be fruitful and multiply," implies not just the parenting responsibility of making babies and raising healthy, encouraged, disciplined children. It means fostering the prospering of life in general. We are to assist the Creator in helping life flourish and become abundantly fruitful. We are called by God to be co-creators with God!

Increasing productivity is not to be seen as simply a monetary growing of financial assets, but rather interpreted holistically as a blessing of life as a whole. It says we are to seek quality of life, not just quantity of life. Environmental responsibility is then basic and intrinsic to our biblical faith. Love of our neighbor cannot be separated from care for our neighbors' lands. This ideal calling was of course made before the incurrence of sin and shame. Their consequences distract, detract, and deter our calling. But they don't deny it! Our deliverance from this polluted mess is thankfully a Messiah/Christ/Savior in whom there is a new creation and a restoration to original goodness. In Christ, there is more than just individual redemption, there is an initiation into the original order of God's garden of paradise!

God's "leadership" in this redemptive venture is described in scripture with various titles, which are metaphors, giving visible imagery to invisible realities. And while God is King of the universe, an authoritarian image emphasized by reformed theology, this title alone neglects the nurturing aspect or role of the divine Spirit. Jesus preferred the term Father. And though we need nurturing fathers and there are too many fathers who are not very nurturing, indeed sometimes even absent or abusive, this is a good reason to embrace a "good father" image and role model of God. I believe that the Good Shepherd King is a good title that emphasizes the providential care of guiding, feeding, and protecting.

There are other agricultural images from Jesus's parables of the vineyard where God is the owner/master, and Christ the son/heir. Jesus referred to Himself as the True Vine that feeds His disciples who are the branches that bear much fruit. His followers are also called to be laborers in the vineyard. At any rate, we are nurtured and called to nurture others as Christ does by word and spirit, wisdom and warmth, truth and grace. And although God is the Complete, Cosmic, Constant Gardener, the Final Farmer, we as imitators made in His image are meant to share in the leadership enterprise of this Ultimate Aggie, enhancing the harvest of a more just and prosperous society.

Building

The second tradition of mechanics or engineering is related to the first of agriculture, and more so originally. It supplements our tradition of growing with the tradition of building. It appeals to our God-given gift of reason to apply scientific logic and technology to meet needs and resolve problems. It sees science as a friend and not just an enemy, though it can and has been misused as such (think creating and proliferating more destructive weapons: manufacturers lobbying for gun deregulation, unnecessary wars and non-redemptive violence).

On our trip to the Holy Lands, our guide pointed out that in the Gospels, the word for Jesus's early vocation was usually misinterpreted as "carpenter," but more accurately translated as "builder"! "That," he claimed, "explained why in that rocky country Jesus would have worked not only with wood, but also with stone, more like a contemporary contractor." He said that it helped explain Jesus' many references to rocks. In addition, the guide suggested that He would have been not slight of build as often depicted, but at least somewhat muscular, if not outstandingly strong!

So the Aggie traditions of engineering or construction science follow in His footsteps as a "builder." Some relevant biblical illustrations include the need for calculating/estimating the cost of a tower, proper planning for a home's foundation, a wealthy farmer preoccupied with financial profit who wasted his life by obsessively building bigger barns, etc. Jesus understood that problem solving skills, which were mathematical and scientific, are relevant to spiritual wisdom and maturity.

As a boy I sometimes found it difficult to feel very close to my engineer dad. One exception was a few days with him, on my mother's insistence, during his construction job near Gonzales, Texas, where he supervised the building of a bridge on Highway 90. My brother Bobby and I enjoyed playing Tarzan on the vines along the river bank. Dad was fairly patient with us, even when Bobby fell into the shallow creek. Dad even took us to the state park and local cattle auction there. He took time to explain the work of the CCC, President Roosevelt's Civilian Conservation Corps, which provided jobs to thousands of unemployed men during the Great Depression of his boyhood. I admired Dad as he used his civil engineering education and Aggie leadership training to build that significant aid to society (part of President Eisenhower's plan for infrastructure). Later in his life, I was proud that Dad also was trusted to be the chief engineer for the Alaska pipeline, bridging the considerable distance from Prudhoe Bay to the main forty-eight states. And I was honored that he asked me for my ideas and opinions about his ideas to make that engineering project work in the midst of a very harsh and changing environment.

But as a young man studying mechanical engineering at Texas A&M and then as a young army officer during the Vietnam War, I felt that God was calling me to join in an even more significant assist to humanity by going into "spiritual engineering," giving my life to help connect people to God, Christ's Gospel, and one another! And God has blessed my life to build pipelines of peace and love, bridges from truth to triumph, and from isolation to communication, and highways from fear to faith! What a joy for example to have encouraged the Aggie women's basketball team (and other men's and women's teams) these last eleven seasons and watch them go from worst to first, from the outhouse to the penthouse, from chumps to champs! Building Champions is a big part of God's and A&M's construction plan.

Fighting/Overcoming

Besides A&M's agricultural and mechanical traditions, it has always held proud it's tradition of military, and when necessary, of fighting to defend safety, justice, and freedom. Aggies have a rich heritage of giving honorable leadership to our country's call to protect and defend against aggression. Perhaps its finest moment of acting on this expression of greater love was its contribution against the evils of the Nazi Axis during World War II when Texas A&M provided more officers than any other school. Until the year before I came to A&M, the undergraduate school was basically all Corps of Cadets. It has since been voluntary, and with the change from a draft to a voluntary United States military in the mid-seventies, it has become a smaller fraction of the total student enrollment. Yet it continues to be a "Keeper of the Spirit," especially since it is a guardian of the Aggie Traditions.

In the Apostle Paul's epistles or letters of the New Testament, he uses the metaphor of fighting to describe the Christian life. He says, "Fight the good fight of the faith; take hold of the eternal life to which you were called and for which you made the good confession in the presence of many witnesses . . . I charge you to keep the commandment without spot or blame . . ." (1 Timothy 6:12–14 portions). Paul makes his statement in reference to the testimony of Jesus Christ before Pontius Pilate and affirms that Christ is the "only Sovereign, the King of kings, and Lord of Lords," i.e., our true and ultimate Commander-in-Chief! This is the inspiration of our traditional Wesleyan hymn, "A Charge to Keep I Have."

Jesus explained to His disciples that if they were to follow Him, they also would need to "take up their own cross." There would always be some resistance to righteousness. In the Beatitudes of the Sermon on the Mount (Matthew 5:1–12), Jesus warns his followers that those who become "peacemakers," i.e., lead persons and society toward wholeness, will become targets of slander and persecution. Baptismal vows of the United Methodist Church invite the decision and commitment to "renounce the spiritual forces of wickedness, reject the evil powers of this world, and repent of your sin . . . to resist evil, injustice, and oppression in whatever forms they present themselves." That makes it clear that our commitment to Christ is indelibly linked to our rejection of sin and all manner of evils! Like the Aggie Code of Honor, we are not simply to live honorably, but also not to tolerate attitudes and actions that are dishonorable! Of course we are to be careful, shrewd in our activism, reform and resistance, but that sounds like we are in for a fight! "Satan prowls and growls like a lion seeking to devour" (1 Peter 5:8). In a way, the good life is not just a path of peace, but also a war full of battles. We do well to remember that we are not to "be overcome by evil, but overcome evil with good" (Romans 12:21).

To win this war and embrace victorious living, Paul encourages all Christians to put on the spiritual armor of God (Ephesians 6:10–20). He names six essential pieces of protection: five defensive and one offensive. And he begins with the belt of truth. Truth is always foundational (remember the Aggie Code of Honor), but especially when we are bombarded with distortions and fabrications: extremists, a wide variety of idolaters and addicts, bigots and hate groups, selfish salesmen, and greedy gossipers! Marketing madness has become mainline. The objective of duplicity is that we become duped! The word fool is both a verb and a noun! We need to secure ourselves from non sequiturs! God gave us the powers of reason and logic. Let us use them for the sake of His kingdom and righteousness. Let us believe the inconvenient truth, and not the convenient lie! Let us not put on our preference for false pride and prejudice, but always put on the belt of truth.

The second piece of armor is the breastplate of righteousness. This means that we protect our heart when we reaffirm our commitment of loyal love for God by following the Lordship of Jesus Christ and His truth and grace, His steadfast love. Believing in Jesus is like wearing a bullet-proof vest! Our hearts are kept safe in Him. Lean on the Lord's loyalty! Let us put on faithfully and wear fearlessly the breastplate of righteousness.

The next piece of godly armor is footwear for readiness in proclaiming the good news of peace. This peace means a wholeness of unity with diversity, that is, without conformity. The speaking in every different language at Pentecost is a precursor to the kingdom of God where there is reconciliation between different ethnicities. Paul has just described in Ephesians this peace as a breaking down of the enmity between Jews (i.e., the true people of God/Jews/Christians) and Gentiles (non-Jews, all other ethnic groups). This enmity or lack of peace is what the story of Babel describes (Genesis 11:1–9). Its resolution is sung by the angels at the first Noel, "Glory to God in the highest, and on earth peace, good will among people" (Luke 2:14). It is described in Acts 2 by Luke as the miracle of Pentecost. This hope and wholeness of change toward inclusiveness is what the Spirit will send our way. Let us make sure that eagerness and preparation to announce this good news is our favorite footwear. Even though Donna and I raised boys, some of the most expensive attire that they requested was costly athletic footwear. Good shoes are very helpful (though sometimes a prop for our false pride). Some historians credit the Roman soldier's sandals with their success militarily. These shoes of Gospel Witness/Teaching (Apologetics) are not cheap, but they are free and are the best way to bring genuine victory/glory to God the Father, Son, and Holy Spirit, and to God's champion children, the Lord's army!

The fourth piece of armor is the shield of faith. Its purpose, says Paul, is to quench all the flaming arrows of the evil one. These sharp, incendiary shafts are usually messages of toxic shame, poison darts of the deceitful Devil. In his strategy of deception and distortion, evil kills with shame. Faith helps us to interpret our circumstances in such a way as to shield us from this destructive shame. Faith helps us admit our mistakes and repent as needed, moved by healthy guilt and shame. But faith also protects our dignity and helps us retain/maintain our honor (self-esteem/healthy pride). With this faith, we can dodge the damage of these darts of disrespect. With this godly armor, we can both shield and shake Satan's shame! Great examples of the many times and ways the scriptures lift up this important function of faith is Psalm 25 and Luke 15.

The fifth piece of spiritual armor is the helmet of salvation. I would tell my sons and players I coached that the two most important "muscles" for any athlete were the ones beneath their ribcage and between their ears: playing well is about heart and smart. As the breastplate protects the heart, so the helmet protects the head. Knowing that we are saved by an Almighty God whose "steadfast love endures forever" safeguards our minds and our thinking! Memorizing and regularly repeating the 23rd Psalm is a great way to refresh one's vision of victorious living, putting on this spiritual hard hat! Wearing this helmet of salvation keeps us confident and restores a healthy swagger of spiritual security, well-being, and poise. Let us not forget to wear this safety helmet as we go out and about! Maintain Agg Swagg! Christianly confident, but not arrogantly cocky! The capital C in Christians stands for Clutch, (Confidence and Courage), not Choke!

The sixth and final piece of armor is the sword of the Spirit, which Paul adds is the "word of God." God's teachings and commandments serve us as an officer his saber: both for defense and for offense and as a sign of honor. They communicate to others the authority that has been bestowed upon us. And so act to prevent attacks from some and gain honor and respect from others. To put on the "sword of the Spirit" means that we need to take time to hear and study the Holy Scripture. Let its wisdom shape our thinking and solidify our believing, guide our living, generate our celebrating, empower our triumphing, and fuel our persevering.

One of the best illustrations of this holy warfare is the debate of Christ and the Devil in the wilderness as Jesus was being tempted after His baptism (Mt. 4:1–11; Lk. 4:1–13). Our adversary Satan is shown to use (misuse) the scripture to enhance his "sales pitch," so we need to see the importance of Jesus and understand and stand firm in the scripture's correct meaning and application. We will need this mature wisdom to refute and reject the Devil's distorted rationale. Failure to remember and reassert the "word of God" is well illustrated in Eve's conversation with the serpent (Genesis 3:1–7). Her half-truth assertion opened the door for temptation. Satan quickly convinced her to ignore God's only command and trespass the wise boundary that God had laid out for them. This unwise warfare, of course, had terrible consequences and casualties, then and still today. So let us take up the sword of the Spirit and the combat training of learning to use properly the word of God for victorious living!

Today, there are many resources to becoming masterful in knowing and using God's word. Those written are available in both paper and electronic versions. Bibles, concordances, dictionaries, commentaries, and many other scriptural resources are available for the many translations and paraphrases. None are perfect, but I tend to trust more the NRSV (New Revised Standard Version). Listening and asking scholarly persons of spiritual integrity and maturity is sometimes best. And even the best scholars will often see things differently in interpretation. But not to worry, like as in other poetry, there are often rich, multi-layered, valid meanings in the verses. Some passages do even conflict with and contradict one another, though usually at the literal level and seldom at the level of major beliefs. Still, pray to know the truth and word and carry the sword of the Spirit. Spirit + WORD = SWORD.

For the true key to gaining "military might" in this spiritual warfare is prayer. Saint Paul concludes his admonition to put on the armor of God with these words, "Pray in the Spirit at all times in every prayer and supplication. To that end keep alert and always persevere in supplication for all the saints" (Eph. 6:18). It is through prayer (and the group/family support of prayer) that we plug into God's power, an energy and insight to overcome our obstacles, a vitality for victory! You would not dream of using your smartphone without daily plugging it into its recharger! So it is for your soul with practicing daily prayer and other "means of grace"! So be sure to develop daily traditions of prayer to plug in your "soul phone" and keep your spirits charged with greater love's positive energy! And remember, life is not an individual but team sport. It takes not only a village, but an army! As ancient soldiers of biblical times often found protection by the defense of linking their shields together (as in the movie 300), so as saints in supplication are we Christians linked together with a huge spiritual arsenal! When we fight the good fight, we are not to fight it alone, but with the assistance of many prayer warriors with shared shields!

At one stretch of the season, senior guard Sydney Carter was experiencing a slump in her shooting the basketball. And though maintaining her top-notch defense, she was being missed by her team on the offensive end of the court. In a close and crucial game, down by two at the end of the game, she found herself with the ball in her hands as her shot clock was running out. With few seconds left, she launched a prayer and then a three pointer to win the game. She told the media afterward when asked about her game winner that she had said a prayer right before shooting. I had encouraged her that she would be coming out of her slump. She told me after a game since then that she sometimes had forgotten her pocket rocks that I had given her. I said, "Sydney, the rocks are just a reminder to pray to a God who answers prayers and is good all the time. The key is to ask Him. With or without the rocks, just pray, and know I'm praying for you!" She said, "Thanks, Brother Barry."

So in our lives as Aggies and/or Christians, we can look to the Spirit and those called by that Spirit, the family of faith and love, to help sustain us in the believer's battles. In the classic hymn, "For All the Saints," we share and are blessed by this song of supplication and prayer of praise:

"For all the saints, who from their labors rest, who Thee by faith before the world confessed, thy name, O Jesus, be forever blessed. Alleluia, Alleluia!

Thou wast their rock, their fortress, and their might; Thou, Lord, their captain in the well fought fight; Thou in the darkness drear, their one true light. Alleluia, Alleluia!

O may thy soldiers, faithful, true, and bold, fight as the saints who nobly fought of old, and win with them the victors crown of gold. Alleluia, Alleluia!

O blest communion, fellowship divine! We feebly struggle, they in glory shine; yet all are one in Thee, for all are thine. Alleluia, Alleluia!

And when the strife is fierce, the warfare long, steals on the ear the distant triumph song, and hearts are brave again, and arms are strong. Alleluia, Alleluia!

From earth's wide bounds, from oceans farthest coast, through gates of pearl streams in the countless host, singing to Father, Son, and Holy Ghost: Alleluia, Alleluia!"

And in the words of the Aggie song, "The Twelfth Man," we share a similar sentiment about the Aggie family or nation:

"When we're down, the going's rough and tough, we just grin and yell, 'We've got the stuff!' to fight together for the Aggie dream; we're the Twelfth Man on that Fighting Aggie Team!"

At a recent reunion of my corps outfits F-1/L-1, I discovered some inspiring history. In 1960, when the new president of TAMC, Earl Rudder, asked for a reorganization of the Corps of Cadets by academic major, one of the twenty-six seniors assigned to the newly formed Company F-1 was asked to design a new corps brass to be worn by all cadets. Cadet Captain Troy Marceleno '60, a bright civil engineering student with artistic talent, charismatic leadership, and a magnificent heart for A&M gathered a team and ideas and then arrived at what is still the present day insignia design. On a shield is a knight's helmet with a crossed saber and fasces holding a banner with the Latin words "PER UNITATEM VIS", which means "through unity strength" (see the Corps of Cadets website with the fiftieth anniversary celebration page or Troy's upcoming book). That same theme of a loyal love (unity) becoming a greater love, greater than our enemy's lies, greed, and hate, armoring us for the victorious living that we hear about in the scripture. From Abraham and Ruth to Jesus and the acts of His disciples, this hope was being lifted up once again as the true strength of Texas A&M and the Aggie family!

Miracle of Incarnation Traditions

Perhaps the greatest of Spirit phenomena is the miracle/mystery of incarnation, which literally means that the divine Spirit becomes flesh. While traditions themselves are a means to make that which is invisible visible, incarnation is the theological term for the breaking into the human experience by God Himself. In the Christian church, the traditional way of recognizing and celebrating incarnation is the ringing of one or more bells. The ethereal becomes sensual, and their ringing brings a musical sense of wonder, joy, and hope.

Because God's Spirit became flesh in a newborn baby in Bethlehem, we celebrate with all kinds of Christmas bells: from silver bells, and jingle bells, to bell choirs and the "Carol of the Bells." Even the incarnational service at Christmas by the Salvation Army's mission giving is summoned by the ringing of bells! Jesus explained that when we serve even the "least of these" in His name, we serve Him. And because Jesus promised to be there where two or more of His disciples were gathered, we ring church bells as the community of faith and love gathers. When a man and a woman become one flesh in holy matrimony, we celebrate their experience of incarnation with wedding bells! At the worship service of the Eucharist or Holy Communion or the Lord's Supper, when the priest announces that the bread is now the Body of Christ, an acolyte ringing a small bell recognizes and celebrates this mystery of incarnation.

Because most people do not know the meaning behind this symbolic tradition, it is a good example of the need to educate folks about that to which traditions point. Similar examples of incarnational traditions is the supplication of God's miraculous power for victory over all obstacles, even death, demonstrated at Easter from the empty cross, from the knocking on wood or crossing of fingers. Most people think it is just a superstitious way to bring good luck, when originally it was a ritual to summon the incarnational strength of God's intervening providence, a sort of prayer for deliverance!

One of our family's Christmas traditions is the purchase and placement of one or more new ornaments for our tree each year. Over the many years, our tree then reminds us also of our history and heritage. There are ornaments that go back to our first year of marriage when we worked on painted pottery crafts together. There are ornaments that our sons, Jason and Matt, made at family Christmas crafts nights. We have ornaments in Southwest décor, which remind us of fun family vacations in New Mexico and Colorado. Photo and craft ornaments by our grandkids represent their beloved place in our lives together. There is even a section of our tree that is maroon and white, with its own rich heritage of Aggie ornament gifts from family and friends. One particular year, we had already purchased a beautiful ornament in Branson, Missouri, where we began the holiday season with inspiring Christmas shows at Andy Williams Moon River

Theater featuring the Lennon Sisters and several others. So we were reluctant to buy any more ornaments. But I decided, with my completion of this book, to add a cloisonné maroon and white Aggie bell on sale at the mall. It seemed to capture what I believe is at the heart of Texas A&M traditions, the Christian faith, and the message of this book. That is to invite the miracle of incarnation into our lives more and more; to ask the power of God's Spirit to set our hearts on fire and guide us to "accomplish abundantly far more than all we can ask or imagine." As followers of Jesus Christ, and as Twelfth Men, the Spirit wants to bless us and others through us. For this, we were made to be conduits of God's encouragement, to make flesh the honors of His truth and grace, the glory of His Greater Love.

Even before the early church and bells, the Judaic community of faith and word was summoned by sound to the presence of God in our midst. It was the blowing of a horn that traditionally announced the entrance of a king, a holy leader, a messiah. As a military school, A&M, with the help of the Fighting Texas Aggie Band, honored the rituals of the horn at morning assembly ("Reveille"), at formation to fight ("War Hymn")(think football and other sports), and to rest ("Retreat" or "Taps"). One of the cherished items that Donna and I brought back from our 1986 trip to the Holy Lands was a shofar or ram's horn bought in Jerusalem. I relished blowing this horn at worship on special Sundays (Christ the King Sunday, Christmas Day, Baptism of our Lord, Pentecost, etc.) that especially celebrate the miracle of incarnation. Like and beyond the bell, it was not only a call to worship, but a wakeup call to unite in Christ, to be attentive to His presence and word, and to "fight the good fight"!

A Final Review

From the earliest days of Texas's first public college of higher education, at a remote, retreat-like setting, in the crucible of military training and academic adventure, with the encouragement of the YMCA and the Christian campus chaplains from various mainline denominations, and strong student leadership of various spiritual backgrounds, and capable Christian presidents, professors, and coaches such as Lawrence Sullivan Ross and Dana X. Bible, there formed at Texas A&M a dedicated community of many cherished traditions. These were an expression of their trust in God's Spirit and the "greater love" demonstrated by Jesus Christ and the followers/friends/family of His faith. They emerged out of the intensive, small group experiences of participation in the Corps of Cadets and the rigors of its military challenge and discipline. The students experienced the joy and effectiveness of unity and belonging; of honor and challenge; and of unselfish service and personal growth in confidence and competence in leadership responsibilities. They also enjoyed the support of various mainline denominational congregations, both pastors and laity. It was much more than book learning. This "other education" was both social and spiritual. It embraced both horizontal and vertical dimensions. And greater challenges, overcome with greater love, helped Aggies grow in greater faith, self-esteem, determination, and a can-do attitude and track record. Aggies felt and believed: "We've never been licked!" And, "Aggies can!"

A&M cadets grew as a band of brothers seeking also to compete athletically with other schools often constituted or organized with less inclusive, more class discriminatory attitudes (for example, depicted in the movies Titanic or The Great Gatsby). These other colleges and universities were called "frat rat" schools and stood in stark contrast to the more egalitarian values of A&M's meritocracy (see the movie We've Never Been Licked). Aggies rejected the lure of shallow status symbols (again think The Great Gatsby or Titanic).

Core values emerged at A&M, which included loyalty, perseverance, excellence, pride and humility, loyalty and unity, courage and leadership, respect and honor, courtesy and hospitality and hard work. They are still available to the Aggies that seek the pure spiritual gold inside the treasure of its traditions. In the short pages of this book, we have looked at these core values of the Christian faith and Texas A&M. We have examined a few of the ways that the traditions help encourage these ideals and a quality of life called victorious living. Jesus urged us to store up these heavenly treasures above worldly glitters. Is this at the heart of your retirement planning? Are these values the purpose that propels your life and legacy?

Throughout my life, I learned to ask three simple questions about the truths I sought to discover, better understand, live, and proclaim. They are "What?" "So what?" and "Now what?" That is to question, "What is this really saying?" then "What relevance does this have?" and finally, "What should I/we do now about this?" The implications of these questions are many. And discovery from this book is more likely in combining Bible study with group discussion and prayer. Find a good group or form one! Wisdom is worth the wrestling. And blessings will abound with wise answers!

I have essentially attempted here to offer you the rock of Jesus Christ, truly the original inspiration for Twelfth Man-ship and the lasting values that Christ represents. I believe these are encouraged by Texas A&M and its core traditions/values and which result in the joy of victorious living. May you grow as a tree planted by the water of His Word of truth and grace (Psalm 1), bearing much fruit as you abide in the True Vine, Jesus Christ. I will pray as well for your building projects: your character, your home/family, your vocation, your community, and your world. The war is yours to win. Grow, build, fight, and pray! Your victorious living and the Kingdom of God is my hope and benediction. Know in God's Spirit that our hope is secured. We are never defeated. We've never been licked!

In the words of Charles Wesley, from what his brother John Wesley called (of thousands of songs he wrote) at Charles's memorial service his greatest hymn, "Come, O Thou Traveler Unknown" (a.k.a. "Wrestling Jacob"):

I know Thee, Savior, who thou art,
Jesus, the feeble sinner's friend;
Nor wilt thou with the night depart,
But stay and love me to the end:
Thy mercies never shall remove,
Thy nature, and thy name is Love!

Lame as I am, I take the prey,
Hell, earth, and sin with ease overcome;
I leap for joy, pursue my way,
And as a bounding hart fly home,
Through all eternity to prove
Thy nature, and thy name is Love!

God bless you with His Greater Love, and gig 'em!

Brother Barry '70

Notes

Chapter 8

Questions for Reflection, Discussion, and Sharing

1. A ritual can help us practice our righteousness (or faithfulness) to God, or loyalty to something else. What is a ritual to promote our loyalty to country, our "patriotic righteousness"? Our loyalty to our Aggie teams? Our faithfulness to a marriage? Our commitment to our children?

2. What are the three r's of religion that promote righteousness? Can you give examples of each?

3. What are some of the most common "never-lasting charms" that people are tempted to lean on? That you are tempted to lean on?

4. What are some family traditions that have taught you good discipline, e.g., manners that have taught courtesy or habits that have instilled a good attitude?

5. How do you understand the connection between environmental responsibility and biblical ethics? Aggie traditions?

6. Can you name any lessons learned from gardening that are life lessons to help you in other areas of nurturing or growing (e.g., friendships, projects, GPA, leadership of groups, etc.)?

7. How is thinking of Jesus as a "builder" helpful? What is something that you have built that you felt good about? What are some things that you hope to build? What are some good disciplines/habits that are important to successful building?

8. A&M is a community that has honored many war heroes as well as heroes of the battlefields of the gridiron, diamond, hardwood, science laboratory, etc. Which are your favorites and why? Which other soldiers or heroes are tops in your admiration? Are they role models? How many have you had a chance to thank?

9. Name the six spiritual pieces of God's armor. Which are the most comfortable for you to put on? Most challenging? Why? How have they helped you?

10. Prayer is the key to the spiritual soldier's footlocker of armor. In the Appendix "Practicing Powerful Prayer," I describe a process of "creating a spiritual IED." Can you describe this in your own words?

11. How do you understand incarnation? Which symbolic traditions inspire you most? Others?

12. "What? So what? Now what?" are three questions you were invited to adopt in seeking wisdom and direction. And with this purpose will come passion and production! What have you learned from reading this book about greater love that you think is/will be most helpful? What difference do you think it can make to your life? What plans would you like to pursue to accomplish this vision?

AFTERWORD

An Introduction to the Appendices and Songbook

In order to fully embrace and enjoy this book and the Aggie traditions and Christian values discussed, I decided to share several related resources not included in the chapters. These appendices will include various prayers, guidelines, acronyms, lists, meeting and journal formats, study suggestions, songs and poems that may better add insight and inspiration, and/or be a practical, relevant resource. With these, I seek to offer scriptural wisdom and spiritual warmth: the power of truth and grace.

My hope is that you may find them helpful in your prayer life, personal relationships, approach to understanding your faith, and strategies for greater effectiveness as an Aggie Twelfth Man, a member of your family or church or team or worksite, a citizen/public leader, or a student or student/athlete!

Many of the songs in the Champion Children of God Songbook were written for daily use in particular situations and at specific times of the day (wake up, meals, before games or other challenges, when washing, at bedtime, etc.) and thus are more helpful if memorized/learned by heart and sung daily as part of your spiritual discipline. My plan is to include the recorded music on my website and perhaps make available a compact disk.

Some of the specific recommendations for the use of these appendices include the following:

- Planning a gathering or series of gatherings to study Aggie Spirit 101: Greater Love;
- Keeping track of your own personal journey of spiritual growth, e.g., journaling, prayer diary, etc.

- Utilizing these resources for a variety of settings, e.g., reunions, high school study groups (perhaps for scholarship applicants), a course for Aggie extended family members interested in deepening their Aggie/Christian ties, a course to recruit A&M students or supporters, an Aggie Moms Club study, a Sunday School class, etc.;
- Other (add your own and share with me/others).

A Word About Specific Appendices

A. **A Prayer of Encouragement** For years I collected passages of scripture that I found very encouraging. I would read over them and meditate and pray about them, which I found very helpful. There were certain Christian writers (too many to name) who stimulated the inspirational effect of these verses and helped me add to my list. A few years ago, I decided it might be helpful to just write them into a prayer that I could and would turn to often. As February of 2011 approached, I decided to polish it and print it on some beautiful floral paper and give it as a gift to the Aggie Women's Basketball team. I made copies for each girl and had one framed for their Bible study area. An additional part of their Valentine's Day card greeting was a pocket/purse rock as a reminder of Jesus's promise at the end of the Sermon on the Mount that "those who hear and act upon my words will be like the wise man who built his house upon a rock upon which the storms would not prevail." From what they shared, their faith became a more important and strengthening part of their successful play/ performances through the National Championship that spring! Later, the Aggie softball team also put this prayer in each locker and found it helpful to access the truth and grace, wisdom and warmth, guidance and energy with which God generously desires to bless us! I pray and trust it will do the same for you!

B. **Home Harvest Ministry** This vision/mission statement helps explain the purpose and passion behind promoting the ministries of worship, outreach, and nurture described in Aggie Spirit 101: Greater Love. Donations and volunteer work for this ministry will support this not-for-profit ministry.

C. **FAITH Acronym** Each morning as I wake up, I pray "Morning Prayer" (song), which lifts up the glorious blessings offered by God's amazing truth and grace, but ends with the often neglected need for us to do our part! This acronym is a resource to remind us that "our part" is a simple yet richly textured thing called "faith" ("by grace you have been saved through faith" [Ephesians 2:8]).

D. **AS101:GL Meeting Format** This outline is a suggestion for those who wish to plan and lead an eight-week course of one-hour-a-week classes. The key is a leadership that exemplifies the Spirit filled and led with a character of honor, hospitality, humility, and helpfulness described in the book. The atmosphere should be relaxed and fun, but also serious and respectful. Bonding with one another, as well as the honored traditions and values, should be a chief goal, something like a graduate course of FISH CAMP. Be creative!

E. **Practicing Powerful Prayer** When Associate Head Coach Vic Schaeffer was announced to take the Women's Basketball Head Coaching position at Mississippi State, I congratulated him and told him how much we would miss him and that I wanted to give him a going away gift of this Appendix. I had heard him refer to the SFT (See it, Feel it, Trust it) process explained in the sports movie "Seven Days in Utopia" as he spoke to an FCA audience, so I wrote up this idea I had been thinking about and gave it to him, explaining the powerful effectiveness of creating spiritual IEDs!

F. **Christian Parenting: Top Ten List** After many years of education and experience in parenting and family ministries including PET (parent effectiveness training), TA (transactional analysis), Friedmann's generation-to-generation family systems theory, and certification to teach AP (Active Parenting), I decided to put together this biblically-based list of parenting priorities. After sharing it on a radio talk show in Texarkana, we had new visitors the next Sunday at the church I pastored, and they asked for it in print! So here it is again.

G. **Conflict Resolution Process ADW** One of Sydney Simon's values clarification strategies was called RDA, which stood for Resent,

Demand, and Appreciate, and was to facilitate resolution of conflicts. Instead, I thought it would make them more difficult to resolve because it seemed to heighten defensiveness and block communication. So I created ADW! And because this is one of the most important tools and skills in establishing and maintaining relationships, I taught it to couples in premarital counseling, parenting, SWTx Conference UMC sexuality courses, and members of my congregations in general. So I include it here.

H. **My Prayer Journal** This form can facilitate reflection and meditation for enriching your personal, family, or group prayer life. Your notes may promote your sharings. You may make copies to be placed in a notebook for a spiritual journal or prayer diary.

I. **Biblical Bipartisanship** There is a time to be conservative and a time to be liberal (Ecclesiastes 3:1-8, John 20:19-23). This reveals some of the Bible teachings as well as our state and country's traditional affirmation of both sides and the need for inclusive and respectful thinking and behavior, patience and flexibility.

J. **Yell Practice Tips for the Twelfth Man** A check list for effective support for your Aggie athletes, outfit members, other classmates/ groups, family members, members of your company, fellow church members, those you teach, etc. In other words, ways to be more helpful in lifting those you lead or who need you.

K. **The Story of Wesley B.** A late breaking account of my nephew and a legend.

L. **The Honor—Shame Intensity Graph** A spiritual engineer's scientific depiction of the relationship of honor and its opposite shame and their relationship to personal and family health. Also depicted is the path from dysfunction and abuse to happiness and effectiveness! This shows the reason it is so important to embrace the honor of affirmation, appreciation, and respect, while learning to avoid treating others and self disrespectfully as unimportant or bad. Learn to add/spread positive energy!

M. **A Fortieth Reunion Prayer** An example you may wish to adapt or use.

N. **Reasons for the Big Event: A Top-Ten List.**

O. **Some Aggie Recipes: Personal Traditions.**

P. **An Introduction to the Last Corps Trip** After I was ask to share this classic poem at the 2015 Master in the MSC, I discovered much confusion and criticism expressed online as to its meaning. So with further research I decided to offer this introduction to help explain its historical and theological context. Any who lead Aggie Musters are welcome to use it.

Q. **Champion Children of God Songbook** Many of the songs I have written over the years and a few others that I have used are included, both for personal enrichment and for use in groups for singing or instruction. Several are prayers that I knew would be easier to remember and use if they were put to music. In many cases, they are recommended for daily use at special times of the day.

The song "Christmas Story" was written late on Christmas Eve of 1984 after I had just found out that my father's cancer was probably terminal, just four years after my mother had died suddenly from a cerebral hemorrhage. I was also in my second year as a pastor to an especially difficult church (ran off five pastors in seven years)!

Several songs I wrote were for the themes of SWTx UMC Conference Youth Camps, where as dean I would put together curriculum and a staff, and lead program including group singing.

Like the "Prayer of Encouragement," I wrote the song "Champion Children of God" first for my personal encouragement and then gave it to the Aggie Women's Basketball Team. Aquonesia helped me teach the girls the tune and hand signs as Donna and I hosted them in our home in 2007. They won their first Big Twelve Championship that next year and went to their first Elite Eight, nearly beating the eventual National Champions, Tennessee! My hope and plan is to eventually have many of these songs recorded for your availability. But the words alone may be used and useful for personal prayer or group inspiration.

Champion Children Of God Song Book

Champion Children Of God

By
Barry Bauerschlag

"We are more than conquerors (champions!) through Him who loved us"
(Rom. 8:37b).
"Finally, be strong in the Lord and in the strength of His power. Put on the
whole armor of God, so that you may be able to stand against the wiles of
the devil" (Eph.6:10–11).

Chorus
Fight the good fight (clap)
Win the victory (clap x3)
Put on the holy armor of God (clap x4)
Fight the good fight (clap)
Win the victory (clap x3)
Holy champion children of God

"Fear not," announce His angels
"The Lord is on your side!"
Like when His Kids left Egypt
His love will turn the tide! So . . .

Chorus
Be brave and know His power
Just like the saints of old
His Spirit will assist you
To make your witness bold! So . . .

Chorus
When fierce becomes the battle
You're tempted to retire
Your God will go before you
And fill your hearts with fire

Chorus
So when your life is loaded
With many a daunting task
Do not become discouraged
All you must do is ask! And . . .

Chorus
Fight the good fight (clap)
Win the victory (clap x3)
Put on the holy armor of God (clap x4)
Fight the good fight (clap)
Win the victory (clap x3)
Holy champion children of God
Holy champion children of God
We are the champion children of God

"Now to Him who by the power at work within us is able to accomplish abundantly far more than all we can ask or imagine, to Him be glory in the Church and in Christ Jesus to all generations, forever and ever. Amen" (Ephesians 3:20–21).

"Who will separate us from the love of Christ? Will hardship, or distress, or persecution, or famine, or nakedness, or sword? . . . No! In all these things we are more than conquerors through Him who loved us. For I am convinced that neither death, nor life, nor angels, nor rulers, nor things present, nor things to come, nor powers, nor height, nor depth, nor anything else in all creation, will be able to separate us from the love of God in Christ Jesus our Lord" (Romans 8:35,37–39)!

Greater Love

By
Barry Bauerschlag

(In the style of "The Beverly Hillbillies")

Aggie humble, Aggie proud
Spirit led to yell out loud
The "Power of Twelve," a cut above
We're honored heirs of "greater love"
Honored heirs of "greater love"

From "Early dawn" and "Reveille"
To "Midnight Yell" done merrily
Maroon and White, we will be true
And always Aggies through and through
Always Aggies through and through

We feel the beat of the Aggie Band
And love the folks of Aggieland
To tried traditions we'll be true
And always Aggies through and through
Always Aggies through and through

We give salute to Rudder and Ross
To Crow and Kimbrough: they were "boss"
To Hargett, Bucky, and our Dat Nguyen
We tip our hats; they're all champions
Tip our hats, they're all champions

To help our teams, our finest call
To cheer them on to "move the ball"
The "Power of Twelve," a cut above
We're honored heirs of "greater love"
Honored heirs of "greater love"

So win or lose, we'll fight the fight
And "stand beside" for Maroon and White
The "Power of Twelve," a cut above
We're honored heirs of "greater love"
Honored heirs of "greater love"
Children of a "greater love"

As Dawns The Day

A Wakeup Prayer

As dawns the day
I start to pray
And hear God say
  His loving plan

(Repeat - optional)

His smiling face
His warm embrace
Amazing grace
  Tells me I Am

                Your smiling face
                Your warm embrace
                Your truth and grace
                  Tells me I Am

His precious child
His creature wild
His servant mild
  Someone who can

                Your precious child
                Your creature wild
                Your servant mild
                  Someone who can!

Defeat the dark
Relay the spark
And reach the mark
Set by the Son

So thank you, Lord
Your living Word
Your mercies heard
  Within my heart

                So thank you, Lord
                  Your living Word
                Your mercies heard
                  Within my heart

These seeds you've sown
These gifts you've grown
Through me be shown
I'll do my part
  Amen, amen, amen, amen, amen!

                These seeds you've sown
                These gifts you've grown
                Through me be shown
                  I'll do my part

"As God's chosen ones, holy and beloved, clothe your selves with compassion, kindness, humility, meekness, and patience. Above all, clothe yourselves with love, which binds everything together in perfect harmony. Let the word of Christ dwell in you richly; teach and admonish each other in all wisdom; and with gratitude in your hearts sing psalms, hymns, and spiritual songs to God" (Colossians 3:12, 14, 16).

Hear My Prayer, Lord

By Barry Bauerschlag

Hear my prayer, Lord
Know that I love You
See that I do
Hear my prayer, Lord
Tell me You love me too
(Create your own prayer verses with four syllables for the first line, such as
"Show the way, Lord"; "Give us hope, Lord"; "Grant us peace, Lord"; "Heal
our hearts, Lord"; "Help us grow, Lord"; "Make me fruitful"; "Organize
me"; "Energize me"; "Help me plan, Lord"; "First things first, Lord"; "Make
me shine, Lord"; "Get me started"; "Keep me loyal"; "Keep me faithful";
"Restore my soul, Lord"; "Fill my cup, Lord"; etc.)

This Little Light Of Mine

This little light of mine, I'm a gonna let it shine (x3)
Let it shine, let it shine, let it shine
Hide it under a bushel, No!
I won't let Satan blow it out!
Shine all over (Aggieland, your home town, the USA, the whole wide world),

God, Our Father

(A round; tune: Are You sleeping?)
By Barry Bauerschlag

Verse 1
God, our Father, God, our Father
Once again, once again
We ask for your blessing, we ask for your blessing
Amen, amen

Verse 2
Christ, our brother....

Verse 3
Sister Spirit, ...

TLC Prayer Song

The Lord is near. Do not worry about anything, but in everything, by prayer
and supplication with thanksgiving, let your requests be made known to
God (Philippians 4:5b–6).

We thank you, God, for your creation
And for the freedoms of our nation
And for our family, home's location
And for the fruits of our vocation

We thank you too for daily ration
As well for hearing supplication
For friends and joy of recreation
And times of worship inspiration

But thank you most for Christ, your Son
Who over evil's battle won
Who walks beside us day by day
Who by His love shows us the Way

So in your Tender Loving Care
We learn to trust and grow to share
And walk by faith to follow where
A home eternal you prepare

A Family Prayer

(May be sung to the tune of Edelweiss)
Words by Barry Bauerschlag

Thank you, God, for the love that you've shown through my family
May your Son, Jesus Christ, always and ever dwell in me
Honor, share, pray, and care: Light of your Word shine on us!
Bring shalom to our home, that we may bring peace to the world!

Butterflies

By Barry Bauerschlag

Butterflies are floating by
Effortlessly touch the sky
Painted by their Father's artistry
Flashing brightly in the sun
Celebrate the victory won
Changes on The Way to being free

CHORUS
Like the butterfly, grace has opened up my wings
Flying way up high, I can hear the angels sing

Colors are all beautiful
Love has filled my cup so full
That I want to share my joy with you
Come and give your life to Him
You will feel new life begin
Trust in Jesus Christ, He will be true

Jesus Christ

(A round)
Jesus Christ, Jesus Christ
He is Lord, He is Lord
He came to save us from all our sin
He is our teacher, He is our friend
He is the beginning and is the end
Jesus Christ, Jesus Christ

Everything Grows With Love

By Barry Bauerschlag

Verse 1 Everything grows with love (x4)

Verse 2 Everyone grows with love (x4)

Verse 3 You and I grow with love (x4)

Verse 4 So pass it on (x3), everything grows with love

Wash Me

Wash me, wash me, wash me with your Spirit (x3)
Wash me with your Spirit, Lord
Cleanse me, cleanse me, cleanse me with your Spirit (x3)
Cleanse me with your Spirit, Lord
Heal me, heal me, heal me with your Spirit (x3)
Heal me with your Spirit, Lord

(Use hand signs with each verse. I: Wash hands, II: Wash face, III: Hands on heart)

Deep And Wide

Deep and wide, deep and wide
There's a fountain flowing deep and wide
Deep and wide, deep and wide
There's a fountain flowing deep and wide

Wide and deep, wide and deep
There's a fountain flowing wide and deep
Wide and deep, wide and deep
There's a fountain flowing wide and deep

(Repeat a few times with hand signs, each time faster!)

Taste The Reign

By Barry Bauerschlag

Skies are dark, but I see the Son
Winds blow cold, but I know Someone
Who can calm the storms and keep me warm when they rage
He anoints my head when the world has hated
His appointments said, "Don't be agitated."
"You are not alone, I Am with you all The Way."

CHORUS
"Come and taste the Reign
Don't give in to fear and pain
Sin and death have all been slain
So come and taste the Reign"

Wearing faith's armor, I can't help but conquer
Breathing prayer's desire, I'll pass through the fire
Where He'll purify me for the world He has overcome
Though powers be there is none like He
Makes my heart to sing for I know He's King
By His risen power, I claim Him as my Lord and my God

CHORUS

All Day Song

(Hand signs are fun and helpful.)

CHORUS
Love Him in the morning when you see the sun a rising
Love Him in the evening 'cause He took you through the day
And in the in-between times when you feel the pressure rising
Remember that He loves you and He promises to stay

Rejoice In The Lord Always

Vss. 2-8 By Barry Bauerschlag

(Philippians 4:4–13)

1. Rejoice in the Lord always
   And again I say rejoice (repeat)

   CHORUS
   Rejoice, rejoice
   And again I say rejoice (repeat)

2. Show gentleness to everyone
   And so you may rejoice (repeat)
   CHORUS

3. Fear not the Lord is coming soon
   And so you may rejoice (repeat)

4. But pray and ask with thankfulness
   And so you may rejoice (repeat)

5. God's peace will guard your hearts and minds
   And so you may rejoice (repeat)

6. Think on the things of godliness
   And so you may rejoice (repeat)

7. Truth, honor, justice, excellence
   And so you may rejoice (repeat)

8. For "I can do all things through Christ"
   And so I may rejoice
   "All things through Christ who strengthens me"
   And so I may rejoice
   CHORUS

   Repeat verse 1.
   CHORUS

The Twenty-Third Psalm Song
(Always)

Vss. 2-5 By Barry Bauerschlag

The Lord is my shepherd; I shall not want. He makes me to lie down in green pastures. He leads me beside still waters. He leads me in paths of righteousness for his name's sake. He restores my soul. Yea, though I walk through the valley of the shadow of death, I will fear no evil. Thy rod and thy staff, they comfort me. Thou preparest a table before me in the presence of my enemies. Thou anointest my head with oil. My cup runneth over. Surely goodness and mercy will follow me all the days of my life and I will dwell in the house of the Lord forever.(Psalm 23: 1-6, NKJV)

V1 The Lord is my shepherd
I'll walk with him always
He knows me and He loves me
I'll walk with Him always

CHORUS
Always, always, I'll walk with Him always
Always, always, I'll walk with Him always

V2 He leads me to good places
I'll walk with Him always
He leads me through dark spaces
I'll walk with Him always

CHORUS

V3 In faithful love, I'm growing
I'll walk with Him always
His grace is overflowing
I'll walk with Him always

CHORUS

V4 From enemies, He'll keep me
I'll walk with Him always
His harvest home, He'll reap for me
I'll walk with Him always

CHORUS

V5 His goodness and His mercy
I'll walk with Him always
To live with Him forever
I'll walk with Him always

CHORUS

God's Own Son

By Barry Bauerschlag
(To the folk tune of "This Old Man")

1. God's own Son
   He loves me
   This He showed upon the tree
   With the grace of an old friend
   He took away my sin
   His gift is free unto all men!

2. Live today freed from guilt
   Upon this rock, Your house is built
   CHORUS:
   Sing a new song to the king
   Let your voices ring
   Praises to the Spirit bring

3. Live today freed from shame
   Glory bound in Jesus's name
   CHORUS

4. Live today freed from fear
   This good news for all to hear
   CHORUS

5. Live today freed from sin
   Time that your new life begin
   CHORUS

6. Live today freed from death
   Life begins with Spirit's breath
   CHORUS

7. Live today freed to give
   (slower) Love's the way we're meant to live
   CHORUS
   Repeat Verse 1

Sleep, Rest

A Christian Lullaby
By Barry Bauerschlag

Sleep, rest
Peace blessed
Angels through the night, Lord
Sleep, rest
Peace blessed
Keep me calm and quiet

Sleep, rest
Peace blessed
Heaven's special soap, Lord
Sleep, rest
Peace blessed
Cleanse our hearts with hope

Sleep, rest
Peace blessed
Angels from above, Lord
Sleep, rest
Peace blessed
Keep me in Your love
They keep me in Your love
Please keep me in Your love

Jesus said, "Take my yoke upon you, and learn from me; for I am gentle and humble in heart, and you will find rest for your souls. For my yoke is easy, and my burden is light" (Matthew 11:29–30).
"Those who abide in me and I in them bear much fruit" (John 15:5b).

Day Is Done

A Christian Lullaby (tune of "Brahms's Lullaby")
By Barry Bauerschlag

Day is done
Night has come
Now I thank you, Lord Jesus

Safe and warm
Free from harm
You're the one who brings me peace

May your light
Through the night
Guide my dreams as I sleep

Find your rest
Truly blessed
By the best I can seek

Jesus said, "Come to me, all you that are weary and are carrying heavy burdens, and I will give you rest" (Matthew 11:28).

"Seek first the Kingdom of God and his righteousness, and all these things will be given to you as well" (Matthew 6:33).

"When it was evening on that day . . . and the doors of the house . . . were locked for fear . . . Jesus came and stood among them and said, 'Peace be with you'" (John 20:19 portions)"

Christmas Story

By Barry Bauerschlag

Long ago and far away
Came a little baby king
The wise men say

Angels sang through the night
Shepherds went to see the Child
Who brought the Light

But here today my heart cries
Broken dreams in darkness seems
The whole world lies

Is that Love born that night
Still alive and shining
In the morning light?

CHORUS
Christmas Story sing to me
Christmas Story bring to me
Christmas glory strong to see
The Hope is still the same!

Candles tell of the Word
Shining in the children's faces
Have you heard?

Good news then Is good news now
So fear not and come to worship
Kneel and bow

CHORUS
Christmas Story sing to me
Christmas Story bring to me
Christmas glory to set me free
To live in Jesus's name
To live in Jesus's name
To live in Jesus's name

O For A Heart To Praise My God

(by Charles Wesley, 1742)

1. O for a heart to praise my God, a heart from sin set free
   A heart that always feels thy blood, so freely shed for me
2. A heart resigned, submissive meek, my great Redeemer's throne
   Where only Christ is heard to speak, where Jesus reigns alone
3. A humble, lowly, contrite heart, believing, true, and clean,
   Which neither life nor death can part from Christ who dwells within
4. A heart in every thought renewed and full of love divine
   Perfect and right and pure and good, a copy Lord of thine
5. Thy nature, gracious Lord impart; come quickly from above;
   Write thy new name upon my heart, thy new, best name of Love!

(Written after his conversion experience and the year before his brother John's. Charles wrote for him somewhat similarly, "O For a Thousand Tongues to Sing My Great Redeemer's Praise.")

Mount Wesley

By Barry Bauerschlag

CHORUS
In Kerrville on the way to El Paso, I'll tell you where my heart longs to go
Friends are really fine; the sun shines most the time: We laugh and sing and worship as we grow
Mount Wesley is the place I want to go!

V1 In the beginning, I was in the dark; I didn't know which way to go
Then God's creation light took me out of the night: Love taught me the things that I should know!
CHORUS

V2 Each one was different, no one felt the same; everybody tried to do his own thing
But as we understood: the Lord's promise is good; in love and trust the Spirit let us sing!
CHORUS

V3 God's peace and joy in fellowship was real; when sharing in acceptance we found grace!
Christ's sacrificial love took Heaven from above: We saw the light of God in Jesus's face!
CHORUS

V4 It seems so long since I started down this road; my burden grew so heavy as I'd roam
Then Jesus came within and took away my sin; now hand-in-hand my Savior leads me home!

Reach One More

(tune: "O God Our Help in Ages Past")
By Barry Bauerschlag

V1 O God of hope and help above
Whose grace is sure and strong
We pray and praise your greater love
Which overcomes all wrong!

V2 Your mercy cleanses us from shame
You cover stain and flaw
Your glory shines in Jesus's name
And gives us cause for awe!

V3 The power of your faithfulness
Restores Your children's nerve
Redeems our joy and gentleness
Rejoicing as we serve

V4 To "reach one more" may grace abound
This goal our God wants most
And know the joy when lost is found
Rejoice with heavenly host!

V5 So to repentant sinners now
This gospel hope we bring
Made more than winners we will bow
And glorify the King!

V6 O God of hope and help above
Whose grace is sure and strong
We pray and praise your greater love
Victorious in our song!

Seasons Of The Salvation Story

CHORUS
Seasons of the salvation story
Turning me around in my mind
Teaching me the ways of God's glory
Leading me home just to find
That the separation was only in my mind
He was there beside me all the time

V1 We began the adventure looking for a light, waiting for the Savior to come
Then early one Christmas morn, a little child was born: Now we dance to the beat of a different drum!
CHORUS

V2 He comes inside the walls to the problems and the pain. He speaks with a heart that knows.
He took our death away when He died that darkened day. They thought that He was done, but He arose!
CHORUS

Then He comes and breathes His Spirit upon me and now I know
That I must go and tell the world He loves us so! I love Him so!
CHORUS

Seed Faith Song

By Barry Bauerschalg

V1 A little seed of love has been planted in my heart
It's been nurtured from above: Holy Spirit from the start
Now it blossoms in His Light, and it bears the fruit of joy and peace

V2 Signs of His amazing grace in the soil of faithfulness
Shines the Son upon my face: shades of godly gentleness
Bear true witness to His might: the rich harvest of a sweet release

CHORUS
Glory to the Gardener of Righteousness
Praise to the Prince of Shalom
Honor to Him who brings blessedness
And Love which leads us home

V3 The miracle of growth comes with trusting in His care
Make a covenantal oath to be yoked to His plowshare
Cultivate the Kingdom Song and to the Lord of Life belong
CHORUS

A Christian Family

By Barry Bauerschlag

What kind of love is always together everywhere you go?
What kind of love will leave you never? Do you want to know?
Who do you talk to when friends have left you; you're feelin' all alone?
Where do you go now when you've got a problem and you need a home?

CHORUS
It's a family, a Christian family!
It's a family, a Christian family!

BRIDGE
It's a mother, it's a father, a brother, sister too.
Laughin', carin', prayin', sharin': it's for me and you!
CHORUS

Rock-a My Soul

CHORUS
Rock-a my soul in the bosom of Abraham (x3)
Oh rock-a my soul

V1 So high, ya can't get over it
So low, ya can't get under it
So wide, ya can't get around it
Ya gotta go in at The Door

CHORUS
Oh yeah now

V2 Rock, rock, rock-a my soul (x3)
Oh, rock-a my soul

The Jesus Journey

By Barry Bauerschlag

V1 When you want to know just who loves you so
You've been walkin' blind, can't find peace of mind
Turn to Jesus, you turn to Jesus
Some may laugh at you, yet you know He's true
For He gives you hope, so you tell them "No"
And turn to Jesus, you turn to Jesus

CHORUS
You have started on the Jesus Journey
And you know you've got a friend on The Way
'Cause He's there by your side, and you know that the ride
Is gonna bring you home someday!

V2 You can share my song, come and walk along
Learn to take His stand, cause He's taken your hand
Now follow Jesus, just follow Jesus
In the midst of wrong, He will make you strong
And though the night is long, you keep singin' His song
And follow Jesus, just follow Jesus
CHORUS and repeat

Families For Shalom

By Barry Bauerschlag

V1 What is a woman, and what is a man?
Who do you need to grow and understand?
Jesus is the Savior who's going to take us home!
Families for shalom. Families for shalom.

V2 How can you learn to live with one another?
Love for your sister and love for your brother?
The way that you want it you must do unto others!
Families for shalom. Families for shalom.

CHORUS
Come alive! In His Spirit, we will be set free if we surrender!
Miracles of His love await God's family; the moment's tender!

V3 The One who made us said, "It's not good to be alone!"
"If you want to build a house you've got to start with the Stone!"
Now it's time to spread the Word around: Jerusalem to Rome!
Families for Shalom. Families for Shalom.

V4 You're invited to a table where the Supper is to share
The family's now gathering, there's joy in the air
There's a place beside the Master if you've faith to really care?!
Families for shalom. Families for shalom. Families for shalom!
CHORUS

Chosen By God

By Barry Bauerschlag

Chosen by God (echo),
Choosing to serve (echo)
Learning to love (echo),
Loving to learn (echo)
Given a gift (echo),
Gifted to give (echo)
(Unison) Chosen by God, choosing to serve, learning to live

FAITH

Our Part in God's Plan

"For by grace you have been saved through faith" (Ephesians 2:8a).

F - Follow Jesus Christ; His teachings, commandments, and example (Mark 1:17)
Trust His amazing grace, believe in the power of His steadfast love. Find courage from His life, death, and resurrection, wisdom from His truth and forgiveness from His mercy.

A - Ask to do God's will; seek and knock for His abundant life, His truthful freedom, His complete joy, His answers to all your needs (Matthew 7:7, 6:33; John 10:10; 8:32; 15:11).

I - Invite the Holy Spirit to illuminate and inspire, indwelling our hearts and homes, and invigorating our witness (Luke 11:13; Acts 4:31).

T - Three T's: Trust in God's love (providing and protecting care) and promises;
Think on these things: truth, justice, honor, beauty, and excellence with a Thankful heart (Philippians 4:8). Give Thanks!

H - Help others to know the truth and grace of our Lord; sharing His love and showing His holiness with acts of authentic kindness and unselfish service (Galatians 5:22, 6:10).

"Not that I have already obtained this or have reached the goal; but I press on to make it my own, because Christ Jesus has made me his own. Beloved, I do not consider that I have made it my own; but this one thing I do; forgetting what lies behind and straining forward to what lies ahead, I press on toward the goal for the prize of the heavenly call of God in Christ Jesus. Let those of us then who are mature be of the same mind" (Philippians 3:12–15a).

What is the most important vitamin for the Christian? B-1 (Be one)!

This is a wonderful description of a Pilgrim's Progress.

A Prayer of Encouragement

(Based on scriptural affirmations; from Aggie Spirit
101: Greater Love by Barry Bauerschlag '70)

O God of our Lord Jesus Christ
Whose steadfast love endures forever
We praise You for your Living Word of truth and grace
Which speaks to us through Your Son
And by the power and presence of Your Spirit

We thank you for Your promises and assurances in Holy Scripture:
That we can do all things through Christ who strengthens us
That all things work for good for those who love You
And are called according to Your purpose
That if we abide in You, we will bear much fruit
And whatever we ask will be done for us
More even than we can ask or imagine!
That as we delight in you,
You will give us the desires of our hearts
You have taught us to ask, and it will be given
To seek, and we will find
To knock, and the door will be opened
For all things are possible to those who believe!

You have told us:
To seek first Your kingdom and Your righteousness
And all the things we need will be added
To let Your joy be our strength
For You enjoy giving good gifts to Your children:
Gifts of heart and home and health and happiness
Your greater love makes the weak strong, and the poor rich
The sick whole, and the oppressed free
For greater is He who is within us

Than he who is in the world
Indeed, if You are for us, who dares to be against us!
We are so blessed in this New Covenant of Christ
As we love, honor, and encourage one another!
Good Shepherd Lord, fill your lambs
Restore our souls, anoint our heads, and lead us in paths of righteousness!

Thank you for the good plans you have for our lives
And Your promise to bring them to completion
For Your favor goes with us
And Your blessings chase us down and overtake us
Great is your faithfulness: You will not fail us or forsake us! Your steadfast love endures forever!
Powerful and generous is Your love for Your children! Indeed, our cup runneth over!
So thank you now for this wondrous gift, through faith in Christ, of victorious living:
New, joyful, abundant, free, and eternal life! Lord, we believe; help Thou our unbelief!
We offer You anew our love and trust, praise and gratitude, hope and perseverance, forever and ever. We will be strong and courageous! We will believe and be brave, belong and bring it, then battle together in face of adversity! Let our light so shine! Let it be according to your Word! Amen and Amen

Practicing Powerful Prayer

Implementing a Spiritual IED
(From Aggie Spirit 101: Greater Love ©2012, by Barry Bauerschlag '70)

A rich tradition at Texas A&M that is exemplified by the Corps of Cadets, but also by its athletic teams, is that of "fighting the good fight." As promised in Joshua 1:5–9, God encourages those God calls to "Be strong and courageous" because God is with us wherever we go, and "will not fail us or forsake us"! We are told in Ephesians 6 to "put on the whole armor of God" (verse 11), including the belt of truth, the breastplate of righteousness, shoes of readiness to proclaim the gospel of peace, the shield of faith, the helmet of salvation, and the sword of the Spirit, which is the word of God. Paul then adds, "Pray in the Spirit at all times in every prayer and supplication. To that end keep alert and always persevere in supplication for all the saints."

In the Epistle of James, this brother of Jesus encourages all followers of Christ who are in need and challenged, to pray, and assures his listeners that "The prayer of the righteous is powerful and effective" (verse 5:16b)!

To win the wars over evil and enjoy the victory of answered prayers, I would like to share the ingredients of this powerful weapon for good, the spiritual IED of Imagination, Emotion, and Devotion:

I - **Imagination**   Pray for a vision of that which you desire, to see clearly in your mind's eye that for which you are asking God to grant; an image/"mental video" of your supplication. See the "next best thing/play/step"! At times, it is very helpful to "write (down) the vision" as we are guided in the prophetic book of Habakkuk (verse 2:2b). Imagine the amazing, the magical and miraculous! Visualize and improvise with this explosive device! Imagine the good **you** want to be by saying, "I am _____ (a talent/God-gift, e.g., clutch, quick, accurate, a strong leader, on time, synchronized, MVP, champion, etc.) by God's grace."

E - **Emotion**   Pray thankfully and joyfully that God listens to our requests and will grant our supplications. Feel ahead of time the happy celebration of God's success. Integrate the strong sentiment of success with the clear vision of victory, collectively "rejoicing with those who rejoice"! Smile! Laugh! Celebrate! (dance, hug, high-five, whoop, etc.) Feel good about the next best thing/play/step as if it had already happened! (This step is key to the programming of our subconscious and accessing/connecting with God's higher consciousness! Yell leaders/cheerleaders can help! Encourage one another!)

D - **Devotion**   Pray that our hearts will be centered on the greater love of God demonstrated in the life, death, and resurrection of Jesus Christ; that our lives will be in "focused faith" with His truth and grace; that our walk and talk will match His will. Trust the Spirit's desire to empower and guide you. Remember: our prayers are more powerful when we are more righteous.

"Rejoice in the Lord always; again I will say, Rejoice! Let your gentleness be known to everyone. The Lord is near! Do not worry about anything, but in everything by prayer and supplication with thanksgiving let your requests be made known to God" (Philippians 4:4–6).

AD normally means "after the Lord" (a good meaning), but the following should be added:

A - **Attention**   Pray always. Stay focused on your IED! Maintain your sight on your goal: the next best thing/play, and the eventual outcome of your success. And maintain that blessed feeling of joy in your hope, as well your faith and confidence in what God can and will do!

D - **Dormition**   Sleep on it! Pray to God before you go to sleep to "guide your dreams" and positively program your subconscious, which in turn will positively guide your behavior. Ask your best friend, Jesus Christ, to stay close, watch your back, and keep you on track; his Spirit to shield us with a "banner of love"! (See "A Christian Lullaby" or "Day Is Done" and "Sleep, Rest" in the songbook).

Yell Practice Tips for the Twelfth Man

Add to the positive energy of your teams, individual athletes, or others, like your children or those you work with, in general those that you have an opportunity and responsibility to give supportive encouragement, by

Lifting, not pushing (Say, "All right! You've got it! You can do it!" and not the sarcastic, "Oh, come on!," and ironic, "I can't believe!")

Celebrate success (knowing even small successes lead to big successes when honored with appreciative celebration and words of affirmation, i.e., ascend the upward spiral of momentum into the zone!)

Shield and Shake Shame (Encouragements like "It's OK! Keep your head(s) up! Shake it off! Stay focused! We're coming back!", i.e., avoid the descending spiral into the choke of shame!)

Avoid Loser Laments (like "You suck!" "Bench the quarterback [kicker, returner, point guard, etc.]!" "Fire the coach!" etc. These are two-percenter loser behavior! etc) People need love most when they deserve it the least! Jesus said, "Those who love the most are those who've been forgiven the most!" Maroon and white is for loyal unity, Grinch green is for envy/jealousy. "Rejoice with those who rejoice; weep with those who weep" (not the usual tempting opposite) (Romans 12:15).

Use first names to honor individuals or affectionate positive nicknames

Give celebrity status treating others as the important persons they are

Use simple "kid" words to affirm others

Show affection and appreciation with appropriate physical touch (high fives, hugs, bumps, etc.)

Use positive tones of voice, not sarcastic or mocking (negative, subtracting) tones

Utilize the "whoop!" as well as applause, whistling, and words of affirmation/honor: Amazing! Awesome! Fantastic!, Great job! Way to work! Way to go! Beautiful! Bravo! Spectacular! Wow! Incredible! Outstanding! Special! Smart! Super! Wonderful! Phenomenal! etc.

Employ appropriate hand signs like the Gig 'em and Wrecking Crew to show appreciation like to the defense for a stop, interception, fumble recovery, sack, or tackle for loss; and to the offense for a first down or big play, etc. A raised fist or first finger celebrates God's power!

Rejoice in the Lord always, and again I say, Rejoice (Philippians 4:4)! "When we're down, the going's rough and tough, we just grin and yell,

'We've got the stuff!' to fight together for the Aggie dream; we're the Twelfth Man on that Fighting Aggie Team!"

Practice Powerful Prayer (create a spiritual IED with imagination, emotion, and devotion; see Appendix E)

View Sports (and life) as the Spiritual Events they can and should be: a witness to the power of God's Spirit of truth and grace! A testimony to the prosperity of His victorious living!

Practice (Coach K's) Principles for Building Champions: 1. Love 'em. 2. Believe in them. 3. Share their vision/dreams. 4. Focus on the next best thing (play, game, action, etc.; Forgive and forget failures quickly). 5. Win or lose, play as a team (five fingers make a fist; a pointed finger of blame or shame has three pointing back at you) Again, Romans 12:15. Be of Christian character).

A smaller crowd is not necessarily a bad crowd if they are loyal and effective in their support! A large crowd is not necessarily a good crowd if the fans are only "fair weather fans" who bring a sense of entitlement and attitude which is critical, condemning, and shame based, whose negativity sucks (the energy from the team)!

Aggie Spirit 101: Greater Love
A Suggested Meeting Format Outline

(For a larger group breaking into small groups)

I.   Set up (Lecture, sound system, power point visuals, chairs, refreshments, music, instruments, handbooks and/or handouts, other resources, etc.)

II.   Greeting ("whipping out"—meet and greet). Use assigned and trained greeters, give guidelines, e.g., find out name, class, hometown/HS, what led you to come to Texas A&M?, greatest Twelfth Man joys and/or memorable moments, favorite traditions, most helpful lessons learned, investments (heart treasures), honoring your fathers and mothers (favorite saints/Old Ags), etc. Sing "Shalom to You," possibly "You Are My Wholeness."

III.   Forming of groups by pairs, quads, then eights (is enough). Play games, e.g., finger add/multiply, rabbit in the bean patch, rhythm, shuffle buns, Do you love your neighbor?, sing the "Aggie War Hymn," etc. Distribute handbooks.

IV.   Announcements and introduction of staff, program purpose, and outline/calendar/schedule. Affirm an interfaith setting, yet . . . embrace the coincidence of core Christian and Aggie values. Light a candle and pray (extemporaneous and written). Explain form/substance, traditions/spirit, the place of rituals, rules, and reasons for righteousness' sake. Basic beliefs: foundational faith, e.g., S=G(Fx), "Let honor be your guiding star," true love, wedding vows, etc.

V.   Speaker(s) share about topics and small groups process in pairs, quads, and eights (e.g., yelling for another; "Love Language"; "Where your treasure is . . . and Aggie investments"; zoological values: sheep, doves, and Reveille). Move from history sharing to values clarification, affirmation, and commitment. Show coincidence between the Christian faith and Aggie traditions. Utilize students (athletes, yell leaders, Cadet Corps members,

RVs), alumni/former students, and faculty resource persons. Present and learn Aggie traditions and Christian prayer songs.

VI.   Share pocket rocks and meaning. Sing "Rock-a-My Soul" with "Saw Varsity's Horns Off." Close with the "Twelfth Man Song." Remind to invite friends, family, etc. Greet goodbye with at least five "holy hugs" or handshakes! Amanda Scarbarough's recommendations is "heart to heart" hugs (left chest to left chest, head to right)!

VII.   Visit and clean up.

VIII. Every fourth meeting or at the end of eight week meeting, a celebration/party (with games, refreshments, and music). Remember the "greater love" that has been shown us with a Love-Feast-type of ritual ("Do this/eat this in remembrance of me.").

My Prayer Journal

Date _____

O, Lord Jesus Christ, may we see (know) Thee more clearly, love Thee more dearly, and follow Thee more nearly, day by day. Amen.

Dear God, Creative Father, Redeemer Son, Sister Spirit of steadfast love:

1) Thank you for speaking to me Your truth and grace

In these scriptures

In these relationships

In your creation

To these issues and needs

Through these resources and settings (Upper Room devotions, Sunday School or worship, etc.)

2) I confess my issues, needs, feelings, conflicts, mistakes, trespasses, debts, sins, etc.:

3) I pray for the needs of others, especially

4) Help me deepen my discipleship through spiritual disciplines, such as prayer, study, witness, service, and conferencing/fellowship:

5) I also pray

My Prayer Journal (continued)

Date

Other Prayer/share areas/ideas:

a) The devotional that spoke most to me
   And the need I have which relates to it
b) The blessings with which God/Christ has responded
c) The verse(s) which have been most helpful to hear
d) The time(s) I felt closest to Christ
e) The times I responded to His call to discipleship
f) The times I denied His call to discipleship
g) What I am learning about God/Christ, myself, and/or others
h) What prayer do I want to speak to this?
i) What action do I want to take from this?
j) Who does God want me to invite to join me?
k) Who does God want me to join?
l) Others?

Home Harvest Ministries of Aggieland

MISSION STATEMENT

The purpose of Home Harvest Ministries of Aggieland is to provide an authentic Christian community for mutual support in spiritual growth as Christ's disciples through heartfelt worship, in-depth Bible study, encouraging fellowship, effective prayer, relevant service, and redemptive outreach. Home Harvest seeks the blessings of God's grace through faithfulness to Jesus Christ, His teachings, promises, and commandments, especially as experienced within our family life, our homes and in our families of faith. We therefore emphasize spiritual growth disciplines leading to scriptural holiness done in the covenant setting of small groups and healthy family practices done in the context of our homes, teams, outfits, etc. Home Harvest honors the best of the traditions of the past to embrace the blessings of the Spirit's presence and engages the resources of today to receive the future goodness of our Father's eternal heavenly home. Home Harvest Ministries of Aggieland specifically seeks to discern, understand, and enhance the lasting Christian values expressed and embraced by the many traditions of Texas A&M University for the redemption of the larger worldwide community.

Jesus said, "I Am the Vine, you are the branches. Those who abide in me and I in them bear much fruit, because apart from me you can do nothing" (John 15:5, NRSV).

"Let love be genuine; hate what is evil, hold fast to what is good; love one another with mutual affection; outdo one another in showing honor" (Romans 12:9–10, NRSV).

"Honor everyone. Love the family of believers" (1 Peter 2:17a, NRSV).

Fortieth A&M Reunion Prayer

(An Example)

Dear Lord and Father of us all:

You have created us in your image to be your family through faith. And so it pleases You when your children reunite trusting You in your Spirit of kindred merriment and gracious hospitality. We give You thanks for all our classmates, spouses, and guests who have gathered here once more in Aggieland some forty years after our student days, and for those who could not be here and yet still witness to the lasting values, which are a part of our tradition, a heritage of honor, and a legacy of greater love.

Much water has flowed under the bridge since we were all undergraduates. We have seen the changes of many seasons: many victories and many losses. With grateful hearts, we praise You that Your constant and redeeming grace has been there for us through it all. For what seems tragic in the temporal becomes triumphant in the eternal. We pray that this weekend be a happy time of healing and hope, a homecoming of hospitality and honor.

Bless us then as true Twelfth Men to be a blessing to others as we relive old memories, share present celebrations and struggles, and envision dreams of good things to come. Grant us generous spirits as we continue to be a part of this great university's service to students and state, nation, and world. Help us always to discern and be directed by Your wisdom, Your Spirit of truth and grace. Guide us in our ongoing call to leadership and service, as we lean on your everlasting arms, and build on the firm foundation of our faith traditions and familiness.

Now fill our festivities to overflowing with the new wine of Your steadfast love that our time together will glorify You as we honor the dignity of our friends around us.

For we ask it in Your precious name,
Forever and ever, Amen

Biblical Bipartisanship

The wisdom of Ecclesiastes 3:1–8 explains that everything has a season and a time. The list includes many opposites, some of which would be considered conservative or liberal, cautious or generous, condemning/vengeful or forgiving. Visiting with another pastor from my class of '70 at a recent Aggie women's basketball luncheon, we laughed at how our church members' human/sinful nature is to want God to be forgiving (liberal) toward our own sins/debts, but just (conservative) when it comes to other people's sins/debts (a true non sequitur of illogic: "Mercy me, justice you")!

In the first book of the Bible, Genesis, fun is made of extreme conservatism and extreme liberalism in the creation account. Either can and do lead to sin as the faulty, exaggerated thinking is lampooned in the dramas between the first woman, Eve, and the serpent; and when Cain tries to excuse responsibility toward his brother, Abel. In the first instance, the reptilian temptation to over-extend the moral requirement is offered, "Did God say you shall not eat from any tree in the garden?" Eve rejects this extreme spin in part, but falls into the prideful and angry trap of the smaller lie of partial exaggeration, "God said, 'You shall not eat of the fruit of the tree that is in the middle of the garden, nor shall you touch it, or you shall die" (Genesis 3:1b–3). God never said we can't touch it! Eve had taken the distortion bait of this craftiest wild creature who then proceeded to set the hook with additional temptations. A similar rejection of moral responsibility is depicted in Chapter 4 when God questions Cain about his brother's whereabouts. Cain's famous reply was, "Am I my brother's keeper?" I learned in graduate Bible study that this was an attempt to avoid responsibility by comparing family relationships to tending livestock! Surprisingly, the obvious answer is "No!" The true question is, "Am I my brother's brother?" to which the answer is "Yes!" We are to care for, not take care of one another! Conservative and liberal are meant to listen to, learn from, compromise, and moderate each other. That means both respect and openness, listening with courtesy, and a willingness to learn and compromise, though with a tough insistence to hear and be heard.

After the resurrection of Christ, Jesus returned to His disciples to bless and send them out as He was sent. He breathed on them and said, "Receive the Holy Spirit. If you forgive the sins of any, they are forgiven them; if you retain the sins of any, they are retained." In other words, Christ has given us the choice and responsibility of choosing when to forgive and when to hold accountable, that is, when to be liberal and when to be conservative. There is a time and place and degree for both!

In the State Seal, which Texas A&M embraces and utilizes for its own seal, the Lone Star in the center is surrounded on both sides by two branches. On one side is the oak branch, which stands for conservative "tough love." On the other side is the olive branch, which symbolizes liberal "tender love." At the bottom, the two branches are tied together with a bow. The obvious meaning is the need of both conservative and liberal contributions to come together to achieve the worthy ideal. (The national symbol of the Eagle holding arrows in one claw and olive branches in the other is similar with conservative–liberal choice and responsibility.) Red and blue are respectively the national symbols for the conservative and liberal. Both are considered important to include in and balance our national and state flags. The white stars, a spiritual symbol of our ideals, interestingly emerge from the blue (liberal) background.

The heart symbol of greater love on the cover of this book also displays this color symbolism and balance, with the blue cross emerging from the white fish inside the red heart!

Knowing when and how to lean left and/or lean right, when to shoulder and share or when to refuse to rescue, when to choose tender love or tough love is vital leadership wisdom for all kinds of leadership: parents, bosses, coaches, athletes, public servants/officials, etc. Maroon is a combination of red and blue.

Top Ten Reasons for the Big Event

1. Sacrificial giving for Texas A&M: "Where your treasure is, there is your heart also!"

2. To give back (or pay forward) to the Aggieland community

3. To be good ambassadors of Texas A&M

4. To honor your mothers and fathers

5. To learn important practical knowledge and skills in gardening and home maintenance

6. To better connect with your Aggie family

7. To grow in teamwork, leadership, management, service, community relations, etc.

8. To practice safety and practical responsibility

9. To enjoy God's creation and the beauty of spring

10. To take a break from studying and get some exercise

Other: Add your own.

Conflict Resolution

by Barry Bauerschlag

ADW—Appreciate, Dislike, Want

A = Appreciate - Ask, affirm, admire what you agree with about the other party's stance or behavior. "Seek first to understand, and then to be understood." (See Seven Habits of Highly Effective People by Stephan R. Covey.)

D = Dislike - using the "I message" formula, explain what it is you dislike and disagree with

I Message Formula: "When you _____, I feel _____ because_____. (In other words clarify the behavior or action which is disputed and then explain how it affects you and how you feel about that, i.e., your emotional response.)

W = Want - Be clear with the other person (and of course yourself first) what it is you want. (This helps avoid passive aggressive game playing.) Then seek a shared compromise solution that is win-win, or where both parties get what they want or most/much of what they want/need.

Christian Parenting

A Top Ten List for Family Leadership
(by Barry Bauerschlag, based on the Ten
Commandments and Great Commandment)

1. Put God first, the Redeemer revealed by His Son, Jesus Christ, the Rock upon which the wise person builds his house (family) on the firm foundation of hearing and acting upon His Word. Reverence His name and nature (steadfast love). Pray His truth and grace will bless your family and your leadership.

2. Remember and keep Sabbath rituals holy, which are for rest, recreation, renewal, family inspiration and instruction, shared worship, and witness. Go to church together and keep in touch with your extended family, both natural and chosen. Seek abundant levels of "quality time."

3. Honor each other. Romans 12:10 says, "Love one another with mutual affection; outdo one another in showing honor." 1 Peter 2:17 says, "Honor everyone!" Express appreciation for other family members by what you say and do. Work at catching your children doing well to reinforce a positive self-concept and strong self-worth. Say "Thank you!" often. Encourage one another with unconditional love. Celebrate each other's gifts/talents and successes; give gifts, but not the bribe of a reward.

4. Respect each other's well-being: physical health, sexual integrity, property, and reputation. Don't even dwell on abusive thoughts, and if you do think them, don't act on them. Respect appropriate privacy. Love expresses itself in respect, which is the foundation of honor.

5. Set aside family time to eat daily, pray before meals, share a family night once a week (at least), celebrate special days (birthdays, holidays anniversaries, etc.), take vacations, and attend special events (games, recitals, performances, graduations, etc.). Plan

and practice balance and boundaries; be disciplined, but also be flexible in creating and taking advantage of opportunities for "quality time"! Share power/leadership.

6. Practice good "active listening": asking, affirming, paraphrasing, giving feedback, listening for feelings and content, etc., and giving clear, direct messages including feelings and eye contact.

7. Practice Christian conflict resolution, seeking first to understand and then be understood. Use the ADW process—appreciate, dislike, want (which employs active listening skills and "I messages") to approach disagreements with respect. Discipline not with punishment, which causes resentment, rebellion, and revenge, but with logical consequences, which teach self-responsibility and self-discipline.

8. Greet one another with sincere affection (holy hugs and kisses) both when first coming into each other's presence and when departing, inquiring into their well-being. This includes saying "Good night" with back rubs, story reading/telling, bedtime prayers, etc. God's love is expressed more powerfully with appropriate touching, gentle/friendly tone of voice, use of first name or positive nickname, childlike language, eye contact, affirmation and appreciation, shared laughter, listening, etc. Do God's "Grace Dance" described in Ephesians 5:21–6:4, promoting mutual leadership and submission. Again, encourage both proactivity and cooperation, leading and following.

9. Set meaningful shared goals that each member blesses, supports, and works toward. This may be done at the weekly family meeting or daily during mealtime or bedtime or even at a special planning time, e.g., New Year. A long trip together can be such a time. Make family life a shared, purposeful adventure. Develop a family vision, motto, and mission statement. Bless each individual member's dreams as well!

10. Practice forgiveness so that the garbage of unforgiven sins/ (transgressions, trespasses, debts) does not pollute your present relationships, attitudes, and activities. Admit mistakes and say,

"I'm really sorry. I truly regret it, and I sincerely apologize and will make amends. Will you please forgive me." and teach your children to do the same. Don't drag up old mistakes; instead, "wash each other's feet" spiritually with the cleansing of God's mercy, the forgiving, gracious nature of God's steadfast love. Shake shame! Celebrate amazing grace that restores honor and celebrity status to one another!

Honor–Shame Intensity Graph

Developed by Barry Bauerschlag from the book, Families
Facing Shame by Marilyn J. Mason and Merle A. Fossom

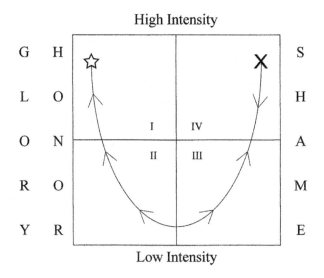

The Redemptive Path is one of de-intensifying and eliminating one's shameful/shaming behavior and embracing and intensifying one's honoring/honorable behavior, moving (clockwise) in general predominantly from Quadrants IV and III and then II to Quadrant I. The shame usually originates with being victimized by abusive/neglectful behavior, then becomes sustained and expanded by dishonorable/dishonoring behavior. Intervention (restoring worth = redemption) is by God's truth (wisdom—also a gift of grace) and grace (love, mercy, generosity). Beware of "backsliding" along the "slippery slope" of counter-clockwise movement/involvement into greater shame. Rituals of redemption include the sacraments of baptism and the Lord's supper/holy communion and a multitude of "means of grace" including prayer and holy fellowship.

A+

Quadrant I – High-Intensity Honor

In this quadrant, a family or group experiences peace, strong performance, and productivity. Loving (patient, kind, gentle, generous, loyal, disciplined, respectful, honest, optimistic, joyful, courteous, enduring, mutually esteeming; see Gal. 5:22 [Fruits of the Spirit]; 1 Cor. 13:4–7 [Love is . . ., love isn't . . .]; mythical symbols: paradise, Garden of Eden [unashamed intimacy]; the Holy City/New Jerusalem [name: Yahweh is our Wholeness/Shalom]; New Creation in Christ; Heaven; the home of champions).

B-

Quadrant II - Low Intensity

In this quadrant, a family or group experiences mild dissatisfaction and moderate performance and productivity. Mildly Polite (emotionally unavailable; neglecting words and signs of affirmation/appreciation/honor; phony, ignorant, undisciplined and/or fearful, cowardly love).

D

Quadrant III – Low-Intensity Shame

In this quadrant, a family, team, or group experiences stronger dissatisfaction, and low performance and productivity. Disrespectfully Rude (arrogant, envious/jealous, irritable, resentful, dishonest/deceptive, selfish, sarcastic, sick humor) and/or Neglectful (ignore, disregard, avoid/dodge responsibility, delinquency).

F

Quadrant IV – High-Intensity Shame

In this quadrant, a family, team, or group experiences severe dissatisfaction and poor performance and productivity. Abusive (verbally/emotionally, physically, sexually, substance, etc. Violently disregarding/violating boundaries, i.e., trespassing, aggressive, intrusive, assaultive, offensive, combative). Why life in a slave culture diminishes family life and persons in it, creating victim and offender shame (of both owners and owned)? Violence/violating begets (births) violence/violating/vengeance. Why "old-school" punishing with violence (versus disciplining with logical or natural consequences) produces the counter-productive three "r's" of resentment, rebellion, and revenge! Mythical symbols: Hell, the outer darkness (with the hypocrites), Babylon, Lake of Fire and Sulfur, sin, the abode of evildoers.

The Story of Wesley Bauerschlag

(and another special Aggie, Jonathan Paul M.)

My two younger brothers, Bob and Bill, both graduated from A&M. Bob (or Bobby as we grew up) married an Alabama girl, Caryl, and they had four beautiful children (Bill and his wife Monica also did). All four have now graduated from A&M, and our family is very proud and thankful for all of them. But we have been especially so of Bobby's second son, Wesley. For Wesley was challenged from birth with the rare disorder of "Prune Belly" syndrome. They were told by their doctors that he would require surgeries and that he could likely not survive, especially to adulthood.

Well, our family had hopes and prayers, and God had other plans! And after student leadership, as a gung-ho bonfire builder, in 2003, before his excited, extended Aggie family, Wes graduated from A&M with an agricultural degree, as had his dad! He was able to find work in San Antonio as a car salesman and did not complain or whine, though I knew it was not the most satisfying job situation. At the time I was doing some substitute teaching. And I shared with Wes that though it was stressful and did not pay very much, there was a great need out there among young people. It was rewarding trying to encourage and educate them, making a difference in their lives. Making an impact!

The next thing I knew, Wes had decided to come back to A&M and get his teaching certificate! In 2007, Wes earned a masters in Ag Ed. He told me that his decision to become a teacher should be most credited to his friend, mentor, and former teacher, the Reverend Doctor Alvin Larke Jr., of Brenham who is an AME Minister and had stood at his wedding as his best man. In no time, we heard that Wes and his young wife, Eileen, had a home in Boerne, Texas, up in the beautiful Hill Country, a half-hour drive northwest of San Antonio, near the Guadalupe River along which his great-great-great-grandfather Bauerschlag used to build homes. And Wes found a job teaching agriculture at a nearby hill country high school. There he enjoyed meaningful relationships, teaching, encouraging, and inspiring youth, which included praising Aggieland. In particular, he had a gifted young man in his classes who was showing much promise and who had accepted a scholarship offer to play ball out of state. Wes continued to encourage him to stay in state and told him that his family deserved to be able to watch him play in college. Wes's example said, "Go to Texas A&M!" And when Jonathan (Hebrew for "God has given") Paul (Latin for "small or humble") Manziel decided to decommit from Oregon and sign with Mike Sherman's Aggies, he invited Wes to attend the special dinner with his new college coach! They have stayed in touch the last few years since.

I remember how excited I was when I watched Johnny's high school highlights on the Internet from his days at Kerrville Tivy. But even more exciting was the spiritual maturity and leadership I saw coming from him in his personal interviews. I knew that his faith and character would bring great blessing to the Texas A&M community and many others. And how happy I was for Johnny, Wes, and A&M when I heard that Coach Sumlin had decided to name Johnny the starting quarterback! "And the rest is history!" as they say, and a pure joy for the 2012 football season and beyond! I said right away that Johnny's leadership of heart and fight reminded me of Bucky Richardson, though with even more faith and talent! And biblically, Johnny Football reminded me of the diminutive David, who not only surprised others by defeating Goliath and the arch rival Philistines, but gave strong leadership to God's people of Israel.

As a pastor in South Texas, I had spent many weeks and weekends in Kerrville as a retreat leader for youth and adults at Mount Wesley (Retreat Center of the SWTx Conference, UMC), seeking to nurture spiritual growth of people from all over that area, both youth and adults and families. Now, we never know what the ripple effects of our faithfulness might help bring, but God promises to bring these blessings! I know while I was there that we, SWTxCUMC, became the only conference in the United Methodist Church to not experience net decline in membership, but grow (especially with the help of the Walk to Emmaus ministries which hold many Mt. Wesley, Kerrville retreats). Unfortunately since I left SWTxCUMC they returned to a decline.

And the cup of blessing keeps running over (see David's Psalm 23, a testimony of David's courage and confidence in God's gifts and guidance)! Well, this last month, (when this was first written) we have just heard that after being told how improbable it was for Wes and Eileen to have kids, she is now expecting, with twins, in May of 2013! Praise God and new medical help! We keep them in our prayers! *P.S. At publishing, Helen and Alice are now two smart healthy and beautiful 2 1/2 year old girls!

Our nephew, Wesley Bauerschlag '03, teacher at Kerrville Tivy High School with Coach Mike Sherman and senior new commitment Johnny Manziel, at the signing dinner, where Johnny had invited him. (See Appendices, "The Story of Wesley B").

Some Favorite Aggie Recipes

(Ideal for tailgate burgers, but great on pork chops, ribs, etc.)

Brother Barry's Special SECret (no longer!) Barbecue Sauce

1 bottle chili sauce
6 tbsp. honey
2 tbsp. molasses
1 bottle/can beer (preferably Shiner Bock)
12 shakes hot sauce (preferably Tabasco)
2 tbsp. soy sauce
2 tbsp. Worcestershire sauce
2 tbsp. A-1 steak sauce
1 lime squeezed
1/2 cup orange juice
1 tsp. brown mustard
1/2 tsp. salt
Montreal Steak Seasoning and black pepper to taste
Plenty for two dozen (12 × 2) Twelfth Man burgers.

Brother Barry's Aggie Tea

Add 1/2 to equal parts of Black Cherry Cranberry juice to your iced tea.

Best with a slice of lemon (or lime for a cherry-limeade flavor)!

Great with burgers (see above), pizza, Mexican food, Italian food, sandwiches (see below), or almost anything!

Brother Barry's Four (or Five) P Sandwich

Pumpernickel (dark), pastrami, provolone, Poupon Dijon, peppers (mild, optional), avocado (optional), purple onion (optional)

Use brown mustard on the meat and cheese side, mayonnaise on the lettuce and tomato side.

May add slices of mild pepper and/or avocado. Great with Aggie tea (see above)!

An Introduction To The Last Corps Trip

for Aggie Muster 2015

Memorial Student Center

Barry W. Bauerschlag '70

The poem, "The Last Corps Trip", was written in the fall semester of 1949 when a large portion of the student body was made up of WWII veterans coming back from fighting the hateful and greedy aggression of Germany and Japan. These heroes had defended our nation and the world from the horrors of Hitler's Holocaust and Hirohito's cruel colonialism, their demons of demagoguery. Aggies had served with courage their country's call to protect her people and the world from this terrible tyranny, the false gods of fascism: Nazi nationalism, racism, and the genocide of its narrow ideology. **All sacrificed some; some sacrificed all!**

These Aggies, these "**Fighting Farmers**", had faced the "Fury" of the good fight and had come through "Unbroken"! Unlikely heroes, not unlike the cinema fantasy, "Guardians of the Galaxy", they had chosen "A Road Less Travelled", and marched to the beat of "A Different Drum"! They rightly believed, "We have Never Been Licked!"

For these veteran Aggies, study abroad had meant the battlefields of the Pacific and Europe. Then in peacetime in Aggieland it meant the downtime of a Corps Trip to Houston, Austin, Dallas or Fort Worth to see friends and family, and watch their beloved Aggie football team battle Rice, t.u., SMU, or TCU. Aggies would often leave a couple of days early to take full advantage of this traditional "R&R"!

So when a professor on a Thursday before a Corps Trip bemoaned a sparse classroom by declaring, "**If you Aggies had a Corps Trip to Hell, you would still leave two days early!**", a student, P.H. "Buddy" DuVal Jr.'51, left that classroom to pen this classic poem which contemplates the Apocalypse, and celebrates God's Final Judgement – **perhaps remembering in Matthew 25 of the New Testament, that this final judgement is reserved for those who have shown the courage of compassion to those downtrodden and disrespected: the poor, the ill, the alien, the vulnerable. When we have unselfishly served these least around us, Christ said we have served Him, and are therefore deemed worthy to receive the eternal blessings of Heaven, the Kingdom of Righteousness!**

This poem was **first read or shared at Bonfire Yell Practice by the Class of '50 Head Yell leader Dr. "Red" Duke!** (That was my dad's senior class, and my first Bonfire at 1 ½ years old. Dad had played football for Aggies Head Coach Homer Norton, and raised me with Aggie Spirit and tradition.) So with pride and passion, and sympathy for the friends and family of those Aggies who have gone before, and especially for those loved ones of the Aggie family who died this last year, before our Roll Call, I share this poem at Muster tonight:

Thirty-two years spent as a pastor: Sharing Christ's love, seeking His wholeness, and making His disciples. (Donna handmade this Lenten stole.) My sons honored me with the nickname "God's Twelfth Man".

Pastor and Wife